100

School Exercises
for Teaching Riding

The teacher must be fully focused on their student, for safety reasons, when teaching jumping.

100
School Exercises
for Teaching Riding

CLAIRE LILLEY

J.A.ALLEN

First published in 2023 by J.A. Allen, an imprint of
The Crowood Press Ltd, Ramsbury,
Marlborough, Wiltshire SN8 2HR
enquiries@crowood.com

www.crowood.com

British Library Cataloguing-in-Publication Data
A catalogue record for this book is available from the British Library.

ISBN 978 0 7198 3501 8

Disclaimer
The author and the publisher do not accept any responsibility in any manner whatsoever for any error or omission, or any loss, damage, injury, adverse outcome, or liability of any kind incurred as a result of the use of any of the information contained in this book, or reliance upon it. If in doubt about any aspect of equestrianism and riding, readers are advised to seek professional advice.

Photos by
Dougald Ballardie

Typeset by Chennai Publishing Services
Cover design by Blue Sunflower Creative
Printed and bound in India by Parksons Graphics Pvt. Ltd.

CONTENTS

The rider's ability to focus on themselves and their horse should be encouraged.

INTRODUCTION

Learning is life-long, whether we are students or teachers wishing to develop and to expand knowledge, learn different techniques, or explore ways of putting things across to pupils. Additionally, self-development in personal qualities, confidence, and lesson presentation skills are of equal importance.

Drawing on my own experience, both as a teacher and a pupil through a long riding career spanning over forty years, this book aims to give ideas for exercises to use in training horses and riders in both dressage and jumping. Training can be enhanced with the use of props, such as ground poles and cones, so exercises that use these imaginatively, to clarify and refine lessons, are also included in this book.

All riding instructors/coaches/teachers are, or have been, riders, so this book has appeal to the teacher wishing to improve their own riding. Even the most experienced top-level riders hone their expertise by constantly improving their horsemanship skills. They do this by re-visiting the basic, fundamental skills of riding, and seek to add interest and value to their own training by putting together different training plans to suit all eventualities.

A rider remembers their first teacher all their life, so the impression they are left with of their learning experience should be positive. To lay a sound foundation for teaching, the Scales of Training are adhered to throughout this book.

As a rider, this book gives insight into what your riding instructor/coach is expecting from you and your horse, and can aid you in preparing for lessons, as well as consolidating prior learning.

The new teacher will learn skills for future development and to ensure their teaching is on track for the student in front of them. More experienced teachers may take on new ideas to incorporate into their teaching methods.

Here, exercises are given for all levels of horse and rider, from novice level to advanced, in both dressage and jumping, including the use of props in training. The intermediate section is aimed at elementary level dressage, with the advanced section from medium level upwards. The aim is that exercises can be combined to create the optimum learning experience for rider and horse, both from a teaching perspective and for solo training – a 'teacher in a book'. The teacher's view – teaching position (TP) – is indicated in the diagrams as a guide as to the best viewpoint for the exercise.

The last section of exercises is for development as a teacher. Suggestions are given to improve teaching technique, such as observational skills of both physical and mental capacities of both horse and rider.

Finally, training plans are given, using the exercises in practice, with consideration as to whether lessons are individual, shared or group, as well as lesson location.

In order to teach safely, attention should be given to the surface being flat, with good footing. An arena is ideal: a 20 × 40m school is adequate for the novice section of this book.

A 20 × 60m arena is recommended, though not necessary, for both intermediate and advanced level exercises, though all exercises given can be adapted for use in both arena and field.

NOVICE DRESSAGE (20 × 40m ARENA)

1. ESTABLISHING DRESSAGE POSITION

Aim of the exercise

Assessing a correct position in the saddle is fundamental to the rider being effective in giving clear aids to their horse, and gives them the opportunity to progress in their skills.

Step-by-step explanation of the exercise

Starting from D on the left rein in medium walk, horse and rider turn onto the quarter line (5m in from the arena edge), halting opposite B (indicated in green). They then proceed on the quarter line, turning left across the arena opposite M. They then track left at H, continue on the track to K, where they turn left again to repeat the exercise.

- ❑ This exercise can be ridden in trot and canter. A change of rein is required to repeat the exercise on the right rein.

- ❑ In order to assess the rider's overall position in the saddle, it is important to view them from the side, head on and from behind.

- ❑ With the side view assessment, the rider should sit tall in the saddle, upright on the seat bones. There should be a vertical alignment of shoulder, hip and heel.

- ❑ When viewed from the front, the rider should appear central to the horse. Check that their knees and feet are level, and that the thighs are in close contact to the horse. Their head should be facing forwards between the horse's ears.

- ❑ From the rear, a clearer view of the torso can reveal further details of any lateral collapse through the upper body.

- ❑ Regarding lower leg position, the upper calf should be on the horse's body, and the feet parallel to the horse's sides. The heels are visible from this rear view, so note if the toes are turning in or out. The stirrups should be hanging vertically.

Common faults and how to rectify these

- • If the rider sits to the rear of their seat bones, this increases pressure on the horse's back under the

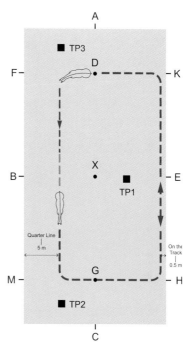

This exercise can be viewed from TP1 to give a side view on both reins, and TP2 and 3 to give a front and rear view.

back of the saddle, and pushes the leg position too far forwards. The alignment of their hips and shoulders should be adjusted, as this will rectify the leg position.

- • With their weight to the front of their seat, the rider will tend to perch on the pommel, loading the horse's withers, which can impinge on its shoulder movement. Their leg position will be too far back. Sitting with their weight evenly distributed in the saddle will place the legs correctly.

- • Should the rider collapse at the waist to one side, this affects their stability in the saddle, with a risk of losing balance, or even falling off. To help rectify this, ensure the stirrups are even, and that the saddle is not over to one side. Assess the alignment of the rider's spine from head to hips and rectify any deviation from the vertical.

2. STRETCHING (WARM-UP)

Aims of the exercise

The aim of the exercise is to promote relaxation throughout the whole of the horse's body by stretching through the back, with freedom of the neck.

Step-by-step explanation of the exercise

Starting from A in medium walk on the left rein, horse and rider proceed to B, where they ride a 20m-diameter circle. On the circle, the rider encourages the horse to stretch through the back, lengthening the reins as the horse stretches forwards and downwards. On returning to B, they take up the contact and proceed around the arena to E, where the circle is repeated. On returning to E, they continue to A to repeat the exercise.

❏ A change of rein is required to ride this exercise on the right rein. Once established in walk, this exercise can be ridden in trot.

❏ Once the rider has lengthened the reins, with the horse taking its neck forwards and downwards for a few steps, ask them to gradually retake the contact. Repeat this give and retake of the reins several times until the rider is at ease with this exercise, without affecting their position in the saddle.

❏ Stretching on a loose rein, with total freedom of the neck, is the ultimate aim, with both horse and rider relaxed and confident in each other. If the rider becomes tense, affecting the horse's state of mind, then the contact should be taken up, and worked again, to aid concentration and re-establish trust before trying again.

Common faults and how to rectify these

• Assess the rhythm of the walk, checking that the rider is not focused on forwardness, going too fast, to the detriment of the regularity and over track of the horse's natural walk.

• It is important that the horse's head and neck reach forwards and downwards towards the ground. If the horse's nose is behind the vertical, there is no beneficial stretch through the back.

• Look for balance and evenness of stretch through the horse's body in both directions. Any drifting

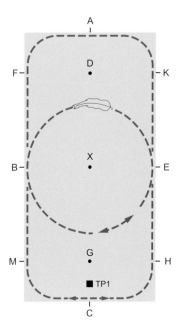

This exercise can be viewed from TP1.

into or out of the circle indicates rider imbalance, so this needs to be addressed. Crookedness in either horse or rider will hinder the horse's ability to stretch through the back and neck.

• Working on a 20m diameter circle is a safer way of stretching the horse, should it be fresh at the beginning of a session. If the horse is unsettled, it is safer for the rider to work the horse calmly in other exercises *before* stretching.

• Observe the rider's position, noticing any tendency to lean forwards as the horse stretches, as this could put the horse out of balance, on its forehand. Their upper body should remain upright, encouraging the horse to step under its body with the hind legs.

TOP TIP

Stretching work is beneficial for mental relaxation, for both horse and rider, when used at regular intervals during a training session.

Stretching work on a long rein is important for relaxation, for both horse and rider, between exercises.

3. STRAIGHT LINES

Aims of the exercise

The aim here is to take an overview of both the body alignment of the horse and the straightness of the rider's posture in the saddle, which impacts on the straightness of the horse.

Step-by-step explanation of the exercise

Starting from A on the left rein in medium walk, horse and rider turn onto the quarter line (5m in from the arena edge). They then proceed on the quarter line, turning left across the arena opposite M. They then track left at H, continue on the track to K, where they turn left again to repeat the exercise.

❏ This exercise can be ridden in trot and canter. A change of rein is required to repeat the exercise on the right rein.

❏ From the front view on the quarter line, check for displacement of the horse's neck to one side, which could be a result of more weight carried on the opposite foreleg, with the effect of drifting to the side through the shoulder.

❏ Viewed from the rear, the horse's hip bones should be level, as should be the rider's shoulders and pelvis. Check whether the rider is sitting equally on both seat bones, and putting the same amount of weight in each stirrup.

❏ The horse's tail should hang vertically. If it is held to one side, this can indicate either tension, or a lack of alignment through the spine. Both sides of horse and rider should mirror each other.

Common faults and how to rectify these

• With straightness issues, mistakes stemming from rider inconsistency can easily be rectified with training. If the horse is not straight, the rider should be corrected first, to see if this resolves the problem.

• An uneven contact affects the position of the horse's head, tipping the nose to one side, with the ears being unlevel. Making sure the rider has equal contact on both sides of the bit can rectify this issue.

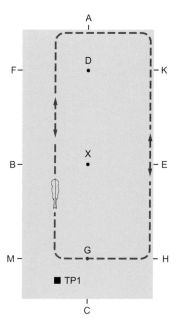

This exercise can be viewed from TP1 to give a front and rear view.

• If the horse's head is unsteady, this is likely to be a result of the rider's hands being too active on the reins, so make sure the rider keeps their hands still.

• Regarding the horse, any deviation of the haunches to one side indicates crookedness. One hip may also be lower than the other, suggesting unevenness of weight on the hind legs. Drifting to either side is indicative of loss of balance, which could be a result of the rider sitting to one side, or the horse being weaker on one side of its body.

TOP TIP

Persistent crookedness, affecting the straightness of the horse, may be due to other factors besides rider technique, so advice from other professionals, such as the vet, farrier or saddler should be sought.

4. TRANSITIONS: HALT/WALK/TROT

Aims of the exercise

The aim here is to improve the quality of transitions between halt, walk and trot, assessing the preparation by the rider for each transition.

Step-by-step explanation of the exercise

Starting from A in medium walk on the left rein, a transition to halt is ridden at the centre of each side, letters A, B, C and E, before proceeding in medium walk.

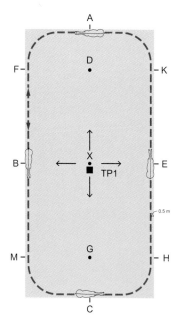

This exercise can be viewed from TP1.

❑ Once the walk-halt-walk transitions are achieved on both reins, progression to transitions halt-walk-trot-walk-halt can be made as follows: with the rider in halt at A on the left rein, ask them to proceed in walk to the middle of the long side. At B, they should proceed to trot.

❑ At C a walk transition is ridden, before continuing to E, where a halt transition can be made. Continue in this pattern, with a transition at each of these letters.

❑ A change of rein is required to ride this exercise on the right rein.

❑ Each transition should be executed as the rider's knee is level with each letter. This is a good test of accuracy in training, but also as preparation for competing in dressage.

❑ The rider's position and balance should be assessed, along with the effectiveness of the aids, and the rider's understanding of how the horse should work through its back into a consistent contact. The better the transition, the more subtle the seat, leg and rein aids appear.

Common faults and how to rectify these

• Lack of forward planning can result in overuse of the aids to active transitions at the letters. The emphasis should be on the quality of the transition, even if the rider overshoots the letter, or is too early in the transition.

• It can be useful to count down the steps into a downward transition, with three half-halts, for example 3-2-1-halt. For an upward transition to walk from halt, if the preceding downwards transition was correct, the horse should be in balance, with sufficient energy to go forwards from a subtle aid.

• When riding a transition from walk to trot, a common fault is to speed up the walk, in anticipation of the trot, with the belief that going faster generates impulsion. If the horse's balance and outline are maintained through the transition, with the hind legs under the body, it is far easier to maintain the rhythm and tempo of the walk, and trot.

TOP TIP

Transition work has a cumulative effect on the horse's way of going. The horse should work in a correct outline relevant for its stage of training, that is a longer, lower outline for a novice horse than for a more advanced horse.

5. CORNERS

Aims of the exercise

The aim here is to develop accuracy and precision when riding corners. Generally, corners connect one movement to another, but taking them as a stand-alone exercise helps to improve consistency of bend, balance and rhythm.

Step-by-step explanation of the exercise

Starting from A in medium walk on the left rein, the rider rides a square, riding through the corner between A and F, turns left at B and E, and riding through the corner between K and A. A change of rein is required to ride this exercise on the right rein.

❏ Assess if the bend of the horse is consistent with the curve of each corner. Each of the corners of the square should be ridden as a quarter of a 10m-diameter circle, connecting to a straight line before and after. Look for accuracy of the line ridden, and how the rider prepares for each corner.

❏ Riding a corner correctly, with the horse in balance, requires the co-ordination of the rider's inside and outside rein and leg aids. This is easiest done in walk, giving more time to make corrections before attempting to ride the square in trot.

❏ Riding this exercise in walk, initially, gives time to correct the technique of the rider, with the aim that the horse improves in suppleness and relaxation as the exercise progresses. Aim for three repetitions of the square before changing direction to ensure even working on both reins.

Common faults and how to rectify these

• Turning too sharply through the corner can happen if half-halts are not used to balance the horse beforehand. The rider may rely on strong rein aids to turn instead of using their outside leg in co-ordination with their hips and shoulder position.

• The horse may fall in off the track after a corner. This can occur if the rider is not supporting the horse through the corner with their inside leg

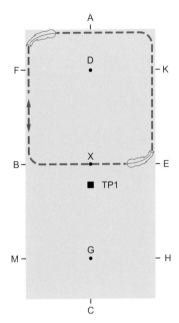

This exercise can be viewed from TP1. Standing on the outside of the square gives a view of both the inside and outside of horse and rider.

and outside rein aids, allowing the horse to fall in off the track. This can be prevented with better preparation, and keeping the horse slightly flexed to the inside (inside position) all the way around the square.

• Variations in rhythm may occur, either by the rider slowing the horse down before a corner in an effort to ride correctly, though this could be a useful teaching point. Speeding up through a corner suggests a lack of care for the horse's balance, so it may benefit the rider to remind them to keep a steady rhythm in an even tempo.

TOP TIP

Learning from this exercise can be applied to the following Exercise 6 and Exercise 7: Circles.

6. CHANGES OF REIN (DIRECTION) ON THE DIAGONAL

Aims of the exercise

The aim of this exercise is to perfect the rider's technique and accuracy when riding the horse from corner to corner, on the diagonal line.

Step-by-step explanation of the exercise

Starting from A in medium walk on the left rein, the rider proceeds to F, changing the rein across the diagonal from F to H. They proceed around the arena on the right rein to M changing the rein from M to K. The exercise can be repeated from A.

❏ Observe how the rider executes the corners at F and M, as they turn the horse onto the diagonal line. Note how they ride into the corner at the end of the diagonal, M and K, assessing the consistency of bend in both directions.

❏ Assess the straightness of the horse on the diagonal, and on the short side of the arena. Watch the lines and how the rider presents the horse onto the diagonal from each of the corners.

❏ Viewing horse and rider from the side on the diagonal line, assess the outline of the horse and the rider's position. Note also the quality of the walk, bearing in mind rhythm and tempo.

❏ Focusing on changes of rein across the diagonal as an exercise addresses any difference in the horse's way of going on both reins, improving suppleness and balance. One of the challenges to the rider is to both accurately bend the horse through the corners, and ride straight on the diagonal lines.

Common faults and how to rectify these

• If horse and rider are unbalanced on the corners, this can affect the overall evenness of the length of stride and rhythm through this exercise.

• Turning too soon onto the diagonal, and prematurely returning to the track at the end of the diagonal – in effect cutting the corners – can be a result of inaccuracy from the rider. To rectify this, make sure they turn onto, and away from, the diagonal when their outside knee is opposite the designated letter, F, H, M and K.

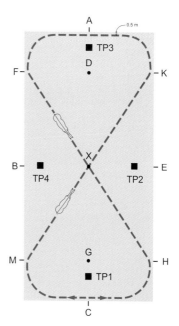

Once the exercise is achieved in walk, it can be repeated in trot.

This exercise can be viewed from TPs 1–4.

• Cutting the corners can also be a result of incorrect use of the supporting aids, namely the inside leg and outside rein. Ensure the rider keeps their outside rein contact sufficient to guide the horse through the corners, but not so firm that it impedes its ability to bend.

• Overshooting the corners can be caused by the rider turning their head, rather than turning their hips and shoulders in the direction of travel, causing the horse to fall out through the shoulder. To rectify this, check the rider's position through the corners, and the effectiveness of their outside rein and leg.

TOP TIP

Changes of rein should be used frequently through training sessions to ensure an equal amount of work in both directions.

7. CIRCLES (20m DIAMETER)

Aims of the exercise

The aim here is to explain the concepts of flexion and bend when riding a 20m-diameter circle.

Step-by-step explanation of the exercise

Starting from A on the left rein in medium walk, the rider commences a 20m-diameter circle, using the four circle points 1–4 (shown in blue) to check if all four segments of the circle are ridden uniformly. On returning to A, horse and rider proceed on the circle line to circle point 2, to ride straight (shown in green) proceeding around the arena to re-join the circle at circle point 4 (shown in green). They then resume the circle at the A end of the arena.

- ❏ A change of rein is required to ride this exercise on the right rein. Once the exercise is achieved in walk, it can be ridden in trot.

- ❏ As a guide, the horse should be on the track for one step when the rider's knee is in line with each circle point. The rider should half-halt at each of the circle points, bringing focus to the horse's way of going, as a check point for outline and balance.

- ❏ The effectiveness of the rider's outside aids should be assessed from outside the circle, which also gives a view of the evenness of longitudinal bend through the horse.

- ❏ A key teaching point is how the horse leaves, and returns to, the track before and after the circle, circle points 2 and 4. Note the rider's concept of flexion and bend, and how they prepare the horse for commencing, and finishing, the circle.

- ❏ The shape of the circle, the balance of horse and rider, and the rhythm of the walk should be observed.

Common faults and how to rectify these

- If the shape of the circle is inconsistent, this can be rectified by asking the rider to halt at each circle point (if riding the circle in walk) in order to maintain the horse's balance through each quarter circle. When riding the exercise in trot, walking a horse's length (three or four steps) at each circle point can ensure the shape of each segment is consistent.

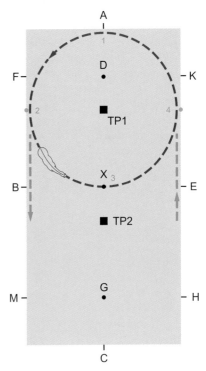

This exercise can be viewed from TP 1 and TP2.

- The rhythm and tempo of the walk or trot may change during this exercise: for example, when commencing the circle the horse may slow down; or it may speed up when leaving the circle to go straight. To improve regularity throughout this exercise, the rider could be asked to count the horse's strides in rhythm.

- If the horse appears reluctant to bend on one rein more than the other, make sure the rider's position is symmetrical and that their aids are equally effective when riding on both the left and right reins, as these can impact on the suppleness of the horse.

TOP TIP

Combine with Exercise 3: Straight Lines and Exercise 5: Corners.

Establishing correct flexion prior to riding a circle.

8. SINGLE LOOPS

Aims of the exercise

This exercise is aimed at improving the suppleness of the horse and precision of the rider's control when riding shallow loops, 5m in from the track.

Step-by-step explanation of the exercise

Starting from A in medium walk on the left rein, a 5m shallow loop is ridden between F and M. A second 5m loop is ridden on the next long side, between H and K. The exercise can be repeated from A. Once achieved in walk, it can be ridden in working trot.

❏ A change of rein is required to ride this exercise on the right rein.

❏ The corner between A and F is ridden with the horse flexed left. Leaving the track as the rider's knee reaches F, horse and rider proceed straight towards a point on the quarter line opposite B, commencing the shallow loop.

❏ As they reach the deepest part of the loop, the horse is flexed right, to return to the track at M. Riding straight towards M, the rider flexes the horse to the left, in preparation for the corner between M and C. They should reach the track as their knee lines up with M, finishing the loop.

❏ A second shallow loop is ridden on the next long side, by inclining from H to a point on the quarter line opposite E, before returning to the track at K, in preparation for the corner between K and A.

❏ Assess how the rider rides through the corners at the A end of the arena, before and after the incline in off the track. They should be ridden to the same depth and the same number of strides taken by the horse through each one. Look for consistency of bend, and the rider's aids to position the horse.

❏ As they incline off the track, check the straightness of both horse and rider. View the change of bend as they reach the deepest point of the loops, opposite B and E. Check again for straightness from this point to the corners at the C end of the school.

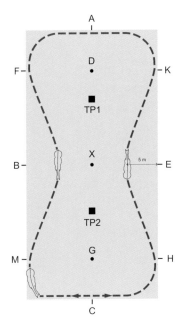

This exercise can be viewed from TP1 and TP2.

Common faults and how to rectify these

• Should the rider be using too much inside rein in an effort to ask the horse for flexion and bend, this can be rectified by the correct use of the rider's inside leg to support the horse through the corners. Make sure they are turning their shoulders in the direction of travel.

• Accuracy on reaching the quarter line at the deepest point of the incline affects the overall shape of the loop, so this needs to be highlighted.

TOP TIP

A more advanced option is to ride the loops in canter, as an introduction to counter canter.

9. FIGURE OF EIGHT

Aims of the exercise

A figure of eight is ridden as two circles that join together. The aim is to assess the uniformity of bend on both circles.

Step-by-step explanation of the exercise

Starting from X on the centre line facing B, in medium walk, a 20m-diameter circle left is ridden. On returning to X, horse and rider proceed onto a 20m-diameter circle right. On reaching X for a second time, the figure of eight is completed.

❏ A change of rein is required before commencing the figure of eight at X with horse and rider facing E. The circle at the A end will be to the left, and the circle at the C end will be to the right.

❏ Once achieved in walk, this exercise can be ridden in trot.

❏ Observe the rider's preparation for the change of direction. There should be a clear horse's length (3–4 steps) on a straight line, the opportunity to change the flexion and bend of the horse from one direction to the other. Check that both horse and rider are straight over X before changing the flexion of the horse to the new direction.

❏ The suppleness of the horse, and the ability of the rider to ride the horse the same both ways, giving 'mirror image' aids, can be assessed from X, being the point where the circles connect, and the bend of the horse is changed from left to right, or right to left. The consistency in shape of the circles should be assessed, along with the bend of the horse, and the rider's position and aids in both directions.

❏ When riding this exercise in rising trot, the rider should change their diagonal over X. In sitting trot, ask for a walk transition just before X, 3–4 steps in walk, and a transition back into trot just after X.

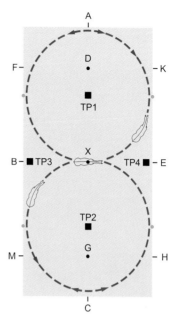

This exercise can be viewed from TPs1–4.

Common faults and how to rectify these

A common mistake is to ride the centre point of the figure of eight as diagonal changes of rein instead of from one circle to another. There should be 3–4 steps on a straight line on the tangent of the circles where the rider changes the bend of the horse. The importance of this can be highlighted to the rider, riding the figure of eight in walk, by asking them to halt at X after the first 20m-diameter circle before commencing the second circle.

TOP TIP

By starting and ending the figure of eight from X, the rider is more likely to ride the change of direction correctly, with 3–4 straight steps on the tangent of the circles.

10. WORK ON A LONG REIN (COOL-DOWN)

Aims of the exercise

The aim here is to work on a long rein a thorough cool-down, to encourage the horse to stretch through its back, aiding relaxation, to ensure a training session ends on a good note.

Step-by-step explanation of the exercise

Starting from A in medium walk on the left rein, a 20m-diameter circle is ridden, with the rider encouraging the horse to stretch forwards and downwards as they gradually lengthen the reins. They then proceed on the long side to the circle point between B and M and ride a half 20m-diameter circle at the C end of the arena. On reaching the circle point between E and H, they proceed straight on the long side to A, completing the exercise. A change of rein is required to repeat the exercise on the right rein.

❑ Once achieved in walk, the exercise can be ridden in rising trot.

❑ Assess the relaxation and stretch through the horse's back on the 20m-diameter circle. Explain the concept of stretching the horse forward and downwards to help the rider to understand the benefits of relaxation for both them and their horse both during and after exercise.

❑ Check the lateral flexion through the horse's body on the half-circle, and the rider's position and balance as they straighten the horse on the long side. The horse's rhythm should not alter as they do this. The rider should be encouraged to guide the horse with their body and not to rely solely on the reins.

❑ A benefit of riding this exercise in rising trot is to encourage looseness and swing through the horse's back. The rider should maintain a supportive rein contact as the reins are lengthened, but not restrict the stretch through the neck. This is also useful during exercises to alleviate any build-up of tension, which is detrimental to the learning process.

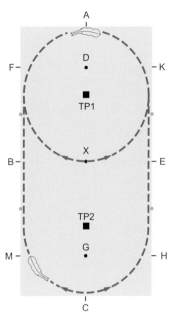

The exercise can be viewed from TP1 and TP2.

Common faults and how to rectify these

• Asking for too much neck bend on the circle and half-circle can result in resistance to the contact, affecting the horse's ability to relax and stretch forwards and downwards. To correct this, the rider should be encouraged to give the horse the freedom through its neck to bend on the circle rather than use excessive rein contact.

• If the contact is dropped, the horse's balance and outline may be affected, resulting in the horse falling on its forehand. Lengthening the reins gradually, while supporting the horse with seat and legs, the rider enables the horse to stretch while taking weight behind.

• If the rider's hand position is too low and the rein contact is restrictive, the horse may come behind the vertical, overbending its neck. Carrying the hands either side of the withers, and making sure the leg aids are effective, encourages the horse forwards to the contact, seeking the bit with its nose forwards and downwards.

NOVICE JUMPING (20 × 40m ARENA)

11. ESTABLISHING JUMPING POSITION

Aims of the exercise

The aim here is to establishing a secure jumping position, essential for the rider's balance and effectiveness when jumping.

Step-by-step explanation of the exercise

❑ Starting on the left rein in medium walk, horse and rider proceed from A to circle point 1 (indicated in blue) following the line of a large circle. They proceed straight on the long side (shown in green), walking over the ground pole at B.

❑ A half-circle is ridden at the C end of the arena, between circle points 2 and 3, before proceeding straight on the long side, walking over the ground poles opposite E. A 20m diameter half-circle commences from circle point 4, returning to A to repeat the exercise.

❑ A change of rein is required to ride this exercise on the right rein.

❑ Once achieved in walk, it can be ridden in trot and canter.

❑ Between circle points 1 and 2 in jumping position, working on keeping their balance on a straight line (shown in green) over the poles. Look for the security of the rider's lower leg position, with the heels down, and the knees close to the saddle. Assess their hip flexibility, core strength and their control over their upper body. Make sure they are able to keep their hands quiet, with a supportive contact to the bit.

❑ On the short sides of the arena, riding a half 20m-diameter circle sitting in the saddle gives the rider a break from balancing in the stirrups.

Common faults and how to rectify these

• If the rider has an insecure lower leg position, they will have difficulty in keeping their balance when standing in their stirrups. This can be caused by their stirrup leathers being too long, so check the

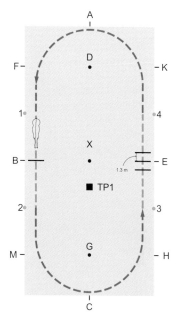

Place a single ground pole on the long side at B on the track, and three poles, set at 1.3m apart on the other long side, opposite E. This exercise can be viewed from TP1, moving on the centre line as required.

rider can balance at the halt before progressing to walk or trot. The rider's toe should be in line with their knee.

• Curving the spine instead of folding at the hip to bring the upper body into a forward position renders the rider unstable, and likely to pitch forwards when jumping. This position often results from instability in the lower leg.

• The rider should be able to ease their arms and hands forwards, to follow the stretch of the horse's neck over a jump. Dropping the contact risks the horse knocking a fence with its front feet, or being unbalanced on landing. Too strong a contact may cause the horse to hollow its back and raise its head when jumping, and may pull the rider forwards out of the saddle in an effort to clear a fence.

12. WARM-UP FOR JUMPING

Aims of the exercise

The aim of the warm-up is to loosen up for jumping. It is useful to ride around jump wings to develop the rider's focus and concentration on accuracy.

Step-by-step explanation of the exercise

❏ Starting from A on the left rein in rising trot, horse and rider proceed on the inside track on the long side between F and M, passing between the jump wings opposite B. Between these jump wings, they commence a large circle.

❏ On returning to the jump wings, they proceed on the inside track, until they are level with the circle point between B and M. Here, they ride a large half-circle to the circle point between H and E, proceeding on the track towards A, going outside the jump wings.

❏ The exercise can then be repeated from A. Once achieved in trot, canter can be ridden on the circle, passing between the jump wings.

❏ A change to the rein is required to ride this exercise on the right rein.

❏ Viewing horse and rider on the circle, from both the inside and the outside, check that they are positioned correctly for maintaining the horse's balance. A side view as they go between the jump wings is useful to check their position in the saddle.

❏ Check the rider keeps the horse straight between the jump wings. Aiming for the centre point between the wings prepares the rider for jumping over the middle of each fence. Rounding off the corners makes it easier for the rider to maintain the horse's rhythm and balance during the warm-up rather than riding corners, which demand more accuracy and a greater degree of engagement. The horse should be ridden on a long rein to establish relaxation and suppleness.

Common faults and how to rectify these

• Going too fast too soon runs the risk of leg injuries for the horse, and a lack of control and balance for

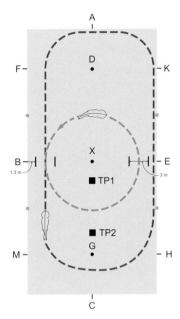

Set up two pairs of jump wings on the long sides of the arena, on the inside track, opposite B and E, 1.3m in from the edge of the arena. From TP1 assess horse and rider from the inside of the circle, and from TP2, the outside.

the rider, neither of which instil confidence. Taking time in walk to relax before trotting or cantering is an opportunity to ensure the rider's effectiveness in guiding the horse, and for them to get used to riding with obstacles in the arena.

• If horse and rider drift to one side when passing between the pairs of wings, this could be dangerous when jumping, as there is a risk of the rider catching their foot on the upright. If the rider is leaning to one side, or if the rein contact is uneven, both would impact on the horse's straightness.

TOP TIP

Horse and rider should be relaxed in trot work before canter is introduced.

Using ground poles is a great way to warm up for jumping exercises.

13. ESTABLISHING LINES OF APPROACH

Aims of the exercise

The aim here is to teach the rider to be accurate when riding towards jumps, keeping the horse straight and aiming for the centre point of the fence, in preparation for jumping. Riding from one fence to another requires as much attention as the jumps themselves.

Step-by-step explanation of the exercise

❑ Starting from A in walk on the left rein, horse and rider proceed straight on the inside track from F to M, walking over the ground pole between the wings opposite B. On the short side, they ride a half-circle line to H, before changing the rein on the diagonal H to F, going over the ground pole between the wings at X.

❑ At F, they pick up a half-circle line around the short side to the inside track between K and H, going over the ground pole between the wings opposite E.

❑ After a change of rein, from M to K, the exercise can be repeated. Once achieved in walk, this exercise can be ridden in trot.

❑ The accuracy of the rider approaching each pair of wings should be observed, and how adept they are at keeping the horse straight, aiming to go over the centre point of each of the poles. Have future jumping skills in mind and check that they plan ahead, giving the horse a clear indication of where to go next.

Common faults and how to rectify these

• A common fault is to cut the corners when changing the rein on the diagonal line between the wings. This has the knock-on effect of putting the horse to one side of the optimum approach line, passing through X. Addressing the rider's technique for riding corners can be of benefit here, bringing their attention to the importance of accurate riding between fences when developing jumping technique.

• If the horse is not kept straight on the inside track, onto the line of approach to the wings, this can

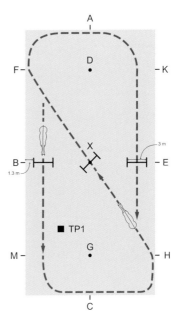

Set out three pairs of jump wings, at 3m apart, at B and E on the inside track, 1.3m in from the arena edge, and on the diagonal line, from H to F, at X. Lay a single pole on the ground between each pair of jump wings. TP1 gives a good viewpoint for assessing horse and rider in both directions.

indicate imbalance in the rider's position, and/or a lack of preparation when riding through the preceding corner. It is important to correct this at this stage, to prevent accidents when progressing to jumping.

• Approaching each pair of wings too fast risks a run out, so the rider should be encouraged to take their time with accuracy as a foundation for jumping later on.

TOP TIP

Setting the wings on the inside track, 1.3m in from the arena edge, tests the rider's ability to ride an accurate line of approach, and not rely on the wall to guide them.

14. BEFORE THE FENCE: THE TAKE-OFF

Aims of the exercise

The aim is to teach the rider to place the horse at the optimum take-off point in trot, in the right speed and rhythm for a successful jump.

Step-by-step explanation of the exercise

❑ Starting from A on the left rein, in working trot, horse and rider proceed around the arena, turning onto the approach line to fence 1. After jumping this fence, they then proceed around the arena, riding a half-circle to the approach line to fence 2. After fence, 2, they continue to A, from where the exercise can be repeated. A change of rein is required to ride this exercise on the right rein, moving the ground poles to the other sides of the fences.

❑ Concentrate on the rider's ability to focus not only on jumping, but on how they ride between the fences, to develop the technique for jumping a course in future.

❑ They should maintain a light forward seat in trot so as not to disturb the horse's rhythm and balance. Sitting to the trot a few strides before the fence helps the rider to get a feel for the movement of the horse's back on the approach, and as it pushes off its hind legs over the jump. The rhythm and length of stride of the trot should be monitored, to ensure the horse is going forwards with sufficient impulsion to jump the fence with ease.

❑ Accuracy is required between the fences, lining the horse up with the centre of each. The horse should take off at the correct point if the gait quality is good, with sufficient impulsion and balance. Concentrating on straightness approaching the fence should be the rider's priority, rather than worrying about the take-off point.

Common faults and how to rectify these

• If the horse is not presented straight to the fence, the horse will be unbalanced and the take-off will

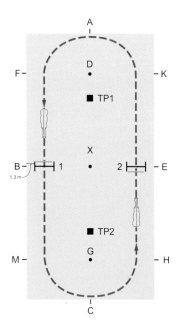

Place a small jump 0.3m high opposite B, with a ground pole 0.3m in front of the fence. Put a second small jump opposite E, also 0.3m in height with a ground pole 0.3m in front of it. Use TP1 and TP2 on the centre line to view horse and rider over both jumps.

be crooked, the weight not equally pushed off both hind legs. This can be rectified by removing the top pole on each fence, leaving the ground poles, checking the rider can ride accurately on a straight line between the jump wings before attempting the jump again.

• Riding too fast towards the jumps impacts on the horse's balance, and accuracy. Ensure a steady rhythm is maintained throughout this exercise.

• An inconsistent rein contact can affect the fluidity of jumping and the horse's forwards momentum, so it is important that the rider maintains a consistent rein contact to guide the horse without unsettling him/her.

15. AFTER THE FENCE: THE LANDING

Aims of the exercise

Focusing on the landing after the fence is the aim here, assessing the balance of horse and rider and their ability to ride forwards after the jump.

Step-by-step explanation of the exercise

☐ Starting from A in trot on the left rein, horse and rider proceed on the inside track between F and M, trotting over fence 1, opposite B. They proceed around the short side of the arena at C on a half-circle to the inside track on the next long side between H and K, jumping fence 2. A second half-circle is ridden at the A end of the school, to repeat the exercise.

☐ A change of rein is required to ride this exercise on the right rein.

☐ When jumping, the rider should fold their upper body forwards from the hip as the horse takes off, and bring their upper body upright as it lands. Keeping their seat in the saddle over the fence helps them to judge the landing point. The point when they come upright in the saddle is when the horse's hind legs touch the ground after the fence.

☐ On landing, they need to concentrate on riding forwards after the jump under control and in balance. Sitting in the saddle a few strides after each fence before riding in a light forwards seat in trot, helps to keep horse and rider balanced as they encourage the horse forwards after the fence.

Common faults and how to rectify these

• If the rider sits upright too soon on landing, before the horse's hind legs are on the ground, they risk being jolted in the saddle, and possibly pulling the horse in the mouth in an effort to keep their balance. To rectify this, ask the rider to keep their upper body folded forwards until they feel the horse's haunches lower after the fence.

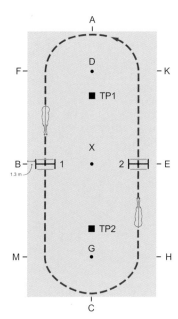

Place one jump at 0.3m in height opposite B on the inside track, and a second at E. Place a ground pole before and after each fence, at 0.3m distance, to focus both horse and rider on the landing as well as the take-off. This also enables both obstacles to be jumped in either direction. TP1 and TP2 are good vantage points to view both take-off and landing over both jumps.

• If the rider looks behind, or turns their head too soon to look at the next fence, this impacts on the horse's balance, so make sure they keep their head straight for the landing. Once the hind legs are on the ground after the fence, they should both be looking to where they are going next.

• If the rider drops the contact over the fence, as a result of leaning too far forwards, they have little steering on landing, and risk the horse stumbling. Check they maintain a steady contact over, and after, the fence.

16. TROTTING POLES WITH A FENCE

Aims of the exercise

The aim here is to establish rhythm, and a straight approach, when jumping from trot.

Step-by-step explanation of the exercise

❏ Starting from A in working trot rising on the left rein, the rider proceeds around the arena following the line of a circle, to circle point 1, riding in a light forwards seat on the long side (shown in green) over the single pole on the track opposite B.

❏ Between circle points 2 and 3, they ride a half-circle at the C end of the school in rising trot. They then proceed straight on the long side in a light forwards seat (shown in green), over the trotting poles and fence.

❏ The exercise can be repeated on the right rein, moving the single fence to the other side of the trotting poles, and approaching from K to H.

❏ Focus on their straightness on the long side, and the speed and rhythm of the trot. Make sure they turn accurately onto the approach, over the three trotting poles and the single fence, taking care that the rider keeps the horse balanced.

❏ Observe the rider's light forwards seat, noting particularly the flexibility of their hip, knee and ankle joints, as they act as shock absorbers to accommodate the horse's movement as it trots over the poles and the jump.

❏ Approaching in trot gives the rider time to focus on their line of approach, lining the horse up with the centre of each trotting pole in preparation for the jump.

Common faults and how to rectify these

• A lack of flexibility in the hip and leg joints can result in the rider's lower leg swinging back, causing them to tip forwards, out of balance. This can be compounded if the rider's stirrups are too long, so they should be adjusted accordingly. An adaptation of this exercise is for the rider to alternate between riding trot and

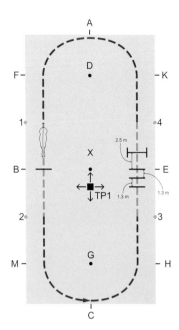

On the long side, opposite B, lay a single ground pole on the track. On the other long side, opposite E, lay three ground poles on the track at a distance of 1.3m from each other. After these, place a jump 0.3m in height at a distance of 2.5m from the poles, to be jumped on the left rein. This distance gives space for the horse to take-off over this small fence after trotting over the poles. This exercise can be viewed from TP1.

a light seat on the half 20m-diameter circles at either end of the school.

• A common fault is for the rider to look at the base of the jump in an effort to gauge the point of take-off, rather than looking forwards over it. Make sure they focus on a point after the fence to ensure they feel when the horse takes off from trot.

> ## TOP TIP
>
> Jumping from trot, rather than canter, means it is less likely the horse will refuse a fence, so this can be confidence giving for the rider.

17. SINGLE JUMPS FROM TROT

Aims of the exercise

The aim of jumping single fences from trot, on the same rein, is to familiarise the rider with jumping from one fence to another.

Step-by-step explanation of the exercise

Set a single jump, 0.3m in height, at the centre point of each side of the arena, on the inside track, 1.3m in from the arena edge, opposite the letters A, B, C and E.

❏ Starting from A on the left rein, the rider proceeds in trot on the long side, turning onto the inside track, lining the horse up with fence 1, on the track opposite B.

❏ The rider proceeds to fence 2 at C, before turning onto the inside track to approach fence 3. They then ride to fence 4 at A, from where the exercise can be repeated.

❏ A change of rein is required to ride this exercise on the right rein.

❏ View the rider over each jump, taking into consideration the lines of approach to each of the fences, and being able to regulate rhythm and balance between the jumps.

❏ Jumping all four fences on the same rein aids relaxation for both horse and rider, without the concern of changing direction. It also gives the opportunity to establish correct bend and balance.

❏ The repetition of jumping in one direction is valuable in the rider learning the technique of bending and straightening the horse between fences to get the best line of approach to each.

❏ Jumping from trot, the horse is less likely to refuse a fence than when jumping from canter, which helps to build confidence when jumping. Sitting to the trot for a few steps before and after each fence ensures the rider's seat is secure, giving them more control over the horse.

❏ Make sure the turns are balanced, and the rider maintains sufficient impulsion in the trot for the horse to jump the fences.

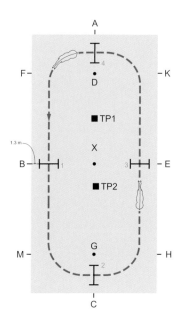

Set a single jump, 0.3m in height, at the centre point of each side of the arena, on the inside track, 1.3m in from the arena edge, opposite the letters A, B, C and E. Starting from A in trot on the left rein, the rider should jump each fence from trot, before changing the rein and repeating on the right rein. TP1 and TP2 give a clear view of the whole arena without being obtrusive to the rider.

Common faults and how to rectify these

• Make sure horse and rider approach the centre of each fence. Drifting back to the track between fences indicates a lack of straightness and balance on landing after each fence. This can be rectified by making sure that the rider maintains equal weight in both stirrups on landing after each fence.

• If the horse is not ridden forwards enough in the trot, it may struggle to jump smoothly over the fences, which could unseat the rider. Ensure the rider rides the horse forwards sufficiently to keep momentum.

• If the horse breaks into canter on approaching a fence, the rider should be encouraged to keep going. Trying to pull the horse out just before a fence might lead to the horse refusing the next time.

18. COURSE RIDING TECHNIQUE

Aims of the exercise

This exercise aims at familiarising the rider with connecting lines of approach when riding from one fence to another.

Step-by-step explanation of the exercise

A simple upright fence 0.3m in height is positioned on the inside track, 1.3m in from the arena edge, at B. A second fence is placed between X and D on a diagonal line from the circle point between H and E, and jumped towards F.

- Starting from A in trot on the left rein, horse and rider approach fence 1, opposite B, and proceed to the C end of the school, keeping the horse straight. On reaching C, a 15m-diameter circle is ridden (shown in green) to ensure a straight approach to the fence 2, at X, on the diagonal line.

- A change of rein is required to repeat the exercise.

- To ride this exercise on the right rein, the fences will need to be changed, with a single fence at E, and the second at X, jumped towards K.

- The 15m-diameter circle will be ridden to the right in the same place, at the C end of the arena.

- Observe the quality, and consistency, of the turns and the straightness of approach to each fence.

- This circle can be repeated as needed, in trot, or in walk if the rider needs a break. It gives the opportunity for corrections to their riding technique, or further clarification of the exercise.

Common faults and how to rectify these

- If the rider focuses too much on jumping the fences, rather than the quality of the trot between them, this could result in a loss of energy before the fence, causing the horse to back off and jump awkwardly. This could be disconcerting for the rider, affecting their confidence. To correct this, make sure the horse is ridden with enough forwardness in trot towards the fences.

- Alternatively, the rider may ride the horse too fast towards the fences, with the horse breaking into

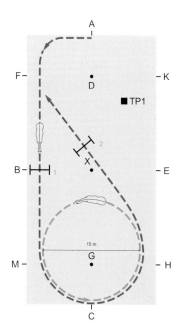

Place a single jump, 0.3m in height, on the track at B. A second fence is placed at between X and D on a diagonal line from the circle point between H and E, and jumped towards F. TP1 gives a clear view of the exercise without distracting the rider.

canter. The circle between the fences is useful here to re-establish control, where the horse can calmly be brought back to trot.

- If the rider has difficulty maintaining the rhythm and tempo of the trot, the top pole of the fences can be placed on the ground, with horse and rider trotting over them. Once corrected, the poles can be replaced, and jumping resumed.

TOP TIP

Riding a circle between the fences gives the rider the opportunity to correct the horse's bend and balance before approaching the fence on the diagonal line.

19. SIMPLE COURSE IN TROT

Aims of the exercise

The aim here is to bring together all techniques in jumping, lines of approach, take-off and landing, speed and rhythm.

Step-by-step explanation of the exercise

Starting in trot on the left rein from K, horse and rider jump fence 1 at A, proceeding to fence 2. After they ride through the short side of the arena at C, they turn on the approach line to fence 3, riding towards F, and turning to jump fence 4, on the right rein.

- They then proceed towards fence 5, riding straight on the diagonal line towards M. After riding through the short side at C on the left rein, fence 6, at E, concludes the course.

- Before they start the course, make sure the horse has sufficient impulsion and balance, the trot has rhythm and that both horse and rider are relaxed. Keeping both horse and rider calm is most important.

- A circle of 15 or 20m in diameter can be ridden at the C end of the school if horse and rider need to regain balance, rhythm, or confidence, between the fences.

- Observe the lines of approach to all fences, ensuring horse and rider aim straight towards the centre of each fence in order for the horse to jump cleanly. This also ensures a good take-off and landing over each fence.

- On the short side of the arena, they should ride a half-circle, which gives an easier option to set up the approach than trying to ride corners before and after C. After fence 6, the rider should bring the horse to walk, relaxing on a long rein.

Common faults and how to rectify these

- When riding on the diagonal after fence 3, make sure the rider plans ahead to the turn to fence 4. Cutting the corner at F would affect the straightness of the approach to this fence, possibly risking a run-out. For this reason, bring the rider's focus to riding a balanced turn, not turning too sharply, giving the horse sufficient preparation before jumping fence 4.

- Should horse and rider have a problem with a particular fence, it can be jumped a couple of times

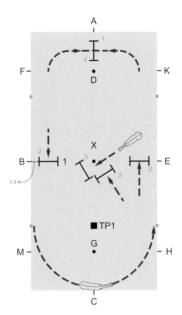

Fence 1 is at A, on the inside track, 1.3m in from the arena edge. Place fence 2 on the inside track, opposite B. Fence 3 is on the diagonal line from the circle point between H and E, jumped towards F. Fence 4 is the same as fence 1, jumped from the opposite direction. Fence 5 is on the diagonal line from the circle point between K and E, jumped towards M. Fence 6 is on the inside track opposite E. TP1 gives a good view of the whole course while keeping clear of the rider's lines of approach.

individually to make the necessary corrections, before resuming the whole course. Allowing space between fences is important for correcting the horse's way of going throughout the course at this stage.

TOP TIP

With the novice horse and rider, keep the number of fences used to a minimum, so they can clearly see their lines of approach. This also allows space to circle between jumps if corrections to a line of approach are needed. Make sure the fences are constructed so they can be jumped from both directions.

A good approach ensures the horse takes off over the centre of the fence.
Photo courtesy of Maisie Morgan Eventing.

20. COOL-DOWN FOR JUMPING

Aims of the exercise

The aim here is to relax and stretch the horse after jumping by riding around the jumps in a light seat.

Step-by-step explanation of the exercise

A 20m-diameter circle is ridden at the A end of the arena on the left rein, and a 15m-diameter circle on the right rein at the C end. Changes of direction are ridden between the jumps, either side of X.

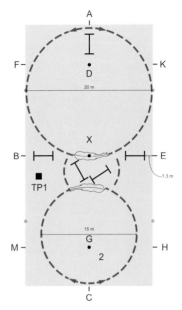

- Starting from A on the left rein, the rider alternates between rising trot and a light forwards seat as they lengthen their reins, allowing the horse to stretch forwards and downwards. The horse should be ridden in balance and working in a steady rhythm.

- Once this is achieved, the circles are repeated on each rein, ending with both horse and rider relaxed.

- Though this is a relaxation exercise, ensure the rider remains focused on the accuracy of the circles, and changes of direction between the fences. It is important for the horse's relaxation that it can trust the rider's guidance from their position and balance as they ride between the jumps.

The fences are placed in the same layout as in exercise 19. The exercise can be viewed safely from TP1, near the jump opposite B, keeps you clear of horse and rider as they ride between the jumps.

Common faults and how to rectify these

- As the rider needs to remain focused on where they are riding during the cool-down, end the session before horse and rider tire. Should the rider lose concentration and get too close to the jumps, they risk brushing against the wings, unnerving, or injuring, both themselves and the horse. Make sure you also remain fully focused on them both at all times.

- As the horse stretches forwards and downwards, the rider should maintain a light contact with the bit, rather than working on a completely loose rein, in order to guide the horse around the fences.

- If the horse or rider become tired, they should ride a transition into walk, and continue to stretch and relax.

TOP TIP

This cool-down can be used as required as relaxation during the jumping exercises to give the horse and rider a break.

NOVICE PROPS (20 × 40m ARENA)

21. WARM-UP

Aims of the exercise

The aim of this exercise is to acclimatise horse and rider to using props in training sessions, developing accuracy and confidence.

Step-by-step explanation of the exercise

Starting from A in medium walk on the left rein, the rider proceeds around the arena, following the line of a 20m-diameter circle from A to circle point 1, between F and B. A half 20m-diameter circle is ridden between circle points 2 and 3, before proceeding on the track to circle point 4. The 20m circle line is ridden, to return to A. From A, horse and rider incline onto a 15m-diameter circle left (shown in green) is ridden around the cone on the centre line. Turning off the track between B and M to the pole on the centre line (shown in blue), horse and rider ride straight alongside the pole, before re-joining the track between H and E.

❏ A change of rein is required to ride this exercise on the right rein.

❏ Once achieved in walk, this exercise can be ridden in trot.

❏ The horse should be in a relaxed outline, with the reins long enough to allow it to stretch forwards and downwards, depending on its degree of relaxation. Using the circle points to ride between helps to develop accuracy, in this instance, when riding from curved to straight lines, and vice versa.

❏ Once they have relaxed around the arena, ask them to ride a 15m-diameter circle around the cone. This circle should be big enough for them to manage on a long rein, by turning with their body, while not getting too close to the cone at this stage. Remember this is a familiarisation exercise. Once they have circled the cone a couple of times, ask them to go large again.

Common faults and how to rectify these

• Each short side of the arena is ridden as a large half-circle, using the circle points, an easier option than riding into the corners as a warm-up.

• Should the horse, or rider, become tense on noticing the pole and cone, ask the rider to keep the horse on the bit to keep control and build their confidence. Once they have both relaxed, the

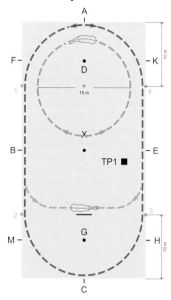

Place a marker, such as a cone or jump block, on the centre line between × and D, in line with the circle points between F and B, and K and E. Each circle point is 10m from the short side of the arena. Lay a ground pole across the centre line between X and G, in line with the circle points between B and M, and E and M.

TP1 gives a view of horse and rider using these, and as they go around the whole arena.

horse can be given a longer rein in order to stretch forwards and downwards.

• In their effort to ride around the cone, and straight alongside the pole, it is tempting for the rider to rely on the reins to turn, so make sure the rider is turning the horse with their body and legs, rather than excessive inside rein.

• Allowing plenty of space for horse and rider to keep a distance from the pole is important in case of inaccuracy in turning.

Encouraging the rider to focus on the contact with the horse's mouth is fundamental to relaxation and a correct way of going when using props in training.

22. USING DRESSAGE LETTERS

Aims of the exercise

The aim is to develop the rider's awareness of the letter placement around the school. This is useful for teaching purposes, so the rider knows what is required and where, and for riding dressage tests.

Step-by-step explanation of the exercise

Starting from A on the left rein in medium walk, horse and rider proceed around the whole school, using the dressage letters as markers. The rider should flex the horse to the left in preparation for the corner between A and F, before straightening the horse for the long side, FM. The corners between M and C, C and H, are ridden before proceeding straight on the long side HK. On returning to A, horse and rider proceed on the centre line (shown in green), noting the letters D, X and G. They turn left at C to join the track.

- ❏ A change of rein is required to ride this exercise on the right rein.
- ❏ Once achieved in walk, the exercise can be ridden in trot.
- ❏ Improving the rider's skill in asking for transitions and movements at a determined point is essential when riding a dressage test. This exercise demands giving clear instructions to the rider to help them think ahead, and to prepare the horse in advance for each movement. Using letters is also beneficial to jumping exercises, using them as a focal point to judge the approach to fences.
- ❏ Look for correct bending of the horse through the corners, and how the rider rides accurately to each letter. Lining up their outside knee with each one when executing transitions, or beginning and ending movements, accurately places the horse at each letter.
- ❏ On the centre line, the rider should be aware that letter D is between K and F, X is between B and E, and G is between M and H.
- ❏ Riding this exercise on both reins ensures the rider can ride with the same precision on the right rein.

Common faults and how to rectify these

- • Often, riders mistakenly assume they are at a letter when the horse's nose reaches it, so to correct this check their outside knee is parallel

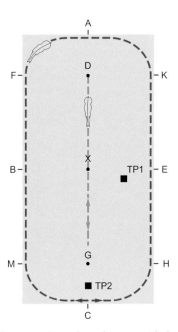

Ask the rider to notice when their outside knee is level with each letter around the arena, so they become accustomed to this. On the centre line, they can look to the long side letters to gauge when they are at the letters, D, X and G. TP1 gives a view of the whole arena. TP2, on the centre line, enables a head-on view of horse and rider on the centre line.

with the letter. On the centre line, they can look to the long-side letters to gauge when they are at the letters, D, X and G.

- • Though this exercise may seem simple, it should not be dismissed as unnecessary, as it is an important way of teaching the rider to use the letters in their training, bringing a sense of discipline in preparing the horse for each movement required in future exercises.

TOP TIP

Make sure the dressage letters are accurately placed around the arena. Expecting the rider to be accurate when the arena is not correctly set up is unhelpful to their progress. See a 20 × 40m diagram like the one above for dressage letter placement. For turning onto, and away from, the centre line, see Exercise 23.

23. CONES FOR TURNING ONTO THE CENTRE LINE

Aims of the exercise

The aim here is to familiarise the rider with turning onto, and away from, the centre line.

Step-by-step explanation of the exercise

❏ Starting on the left rein in medium walk, horse and rider prepare to turn on to the centre line by riding a half 10m-diameter circle from K to D. The cone here is used to help their accuracy when turning the horse on to the centre line. They proceed straight down the centre line, before turning left at G, again with a half 10m-diameter circle around this cone. Make sure the rider prepares the horse for this turn by flexing the horse to the left before G. They then repeat the turn onto the centre line at the A end of the arena.

❏ A change of rein can be made on the centre line by turning right at C, with a 10m-diameter half-circle to the right. They then turn right onto the centre line, at the A end of the school with a half 10m-diameter circle around the cone between F and D.

❏ Once achieved in walk, this exercise can be ridden in trot.

❏ Look for straightness of horse and rider on the centre line. This time, they turn right at the C end of the arena, with a 10m-diameter half-circle right, effectively changing the rein. They then turn right onto the centre line, with a half 10m-diameter circle around the cone between F and D.

Common faults and how to rectify these

• It is common to overshoot the centre line either by turning too late, and omitting any preparation for the turn, or alternatively riding too fast. An attempt to correct this is to ride a crooked line back to the centre line. From a dressage judge's perspective, this would be seen as a lack of balance and bend on the turn, and a lack of straightness on the centre line, both of which would be expensive in losing marks.

• Turning away from the centre line, at C, is also affected by too much speed, and a lack of

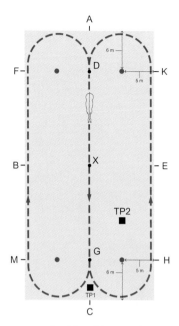

Four cones are required for this exercise, positioned 5m in from the long side wall, on the quarter line, and 6m in from the short side. At the A end of the arena, place one between K and D, a second is placed between F and D. At the C end of the arena, place a third cone between H and G, and the fourth between M and G. A half 10m-diameter circle is ridden around each cone, bringing horse and rider from the long side onto the centre line. TP2 is a good vantage point to see the whole arena, turning as necessary. A dressage judge's eye view can be seen from TP1.

preparation. By keeping the horse straight on the centre line, in balance, and maintaining a steady rhythm, the rider has ample time to plan their turn. If such problems arise when riding the centre line in trot, it can be ridden again in walk.

TOP TIP

Turning onto the centre line with a half-circle is easier than riding into the corners at this stage of training.

24. CONES FOR CORNERS

Aims of the exercise

This exercise uses cones to help the rider to focus on their accuracy when riding corners.

Step-by-step explanation of the exercise

Starting from A on the left rein, in medium walk, horse and rider bend around the cone in the first corner, between A and F. They then proceed on the long side FM, before riding the corners, around the cones between M and C, and C and H. After walking straight on the long side between H and K, they ride the corner between K and A, passing outside the cone.

❏ A change of rein is required to ride this exercise on the right rein.

❏ Once the rider has mastered this exercise in walk, they can repeat it in trot.

❏ To ride an accurate corner, the rider rides a quarter of a 10m-diameter circle around the cone, straightening the horse as they reach F, in order to proceed onto the long side of the arena. The long side gives the opportunity to work on the rider's position, the outline and balance of the horse, and the rhythm of the walk. They should prepare for each subsequent corner in the same way.

❏ The rider's technique as they ride through each corner, bending the horse around the cone in turn, should be assessed. Asking the rider to sit to the trot around the corners maintains focus on their seat.

❏ Well-ridden corners improve the horse's suppleness and way of going, benefiting the horse's balance when turning by engaging the inside hind leg, in particular.

Common faults and how to rectify these

• Turning the horse with the inside rein creates too much neck bend, which can unbalance the horse, causing it to put too much weight on its inside shoulder, and falling in around the corner. Make sure the rider controls the amount of neck bend by maintaining a contact with the outside rein.

• The horse could fall out around the corner if the rider is not supporting the outside of the

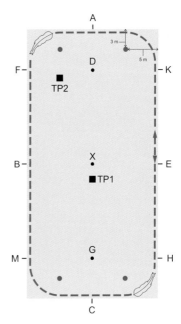

Place one cone in each corner of the arena. They should be 5m in from the long side wall, on the quarter lines, and 3m in from the wall on the short side.

TP1 gives a vantage point of the whole arena, rotating to view each corner in turn. TP2 gives a closer view of the rider's technique as they ride through the corner.

horse with their outside rein and leg. If this is happening, ask the rider to ride a 10m-diameter circle in each corner to give you a view of their outside aids. Once corrected, riding the corners can be resumed.

• A lack of body bend in the horse can stem from a lack of support from the rider's inside leg. Make sure there is sufficient contact with their inside and check for correct shoulder and hip placement around each corner.

TOP TIP

When riding corners correctly, the rider should be able to give their inside rein to test if they have the horse correctly balanced.

25. CONES FOR CIRCLES (20m DIAMETER)

Aims of the exercise

The aim here is to improve the rider's accuracy when riding 20m-diameter circles.

Step-by-step explanation of the exercise

❏ Starting from A in medium walk, on the left rein, ask the rider to flex the horse to the left in preparation for the 20m-diameter circle. They proceed around the cones, returning to A to complete the exercise.

❏ Once this is achieved on the left rein, the rider can change the rein, and repeat to the right.

❏ This exercise can be ridden in trot, once both horse and rider have mastered accurate circles in walk.

❏ Guide the rider around the circle, using each cone as a checkpoint for their position, and the flexion of the horse. View both the inside and outside of horse and rider, to assess both the rider's inside and outside aids.

❏ The accuracy of the circle depends on the rider keeping the horse on the circle line, the same distance away from each cone. By checking this at each cone, the rider is encouraged to focus on each quarter-circle being ridden in the same way.

❏ Sitting trot focuses the rider on their seat and aids around the circle. Rising trot can be useful for concentrating on rhythm. A combination of both, sitting and rising, can be achieved by asking the rider to ride one circle in sitting trot, followed by one in rising trot.

Common faults and how to rectify these

• Riders often turn their head too far to the inside in an effort to look around the circle, which can cause the horse to fall in on its inside shoulder. Check that they look towards the next cone, which ensures that the horse is correctly balanced. The rider's head should be in alignment with the centre of their chest as they ride the circle, looking forwards between the horse's ears.

• When teaching, use each cone as an aid to correcting the rider's leg position. Make sure their inside leg is by the girth, and their outside leg behind. Check their hip and shoulder alignment, and if their hands are parallel. A good test of correct balance, for both horse and rider, is if the rider gives their inside rein forwards for one stride at each cone.

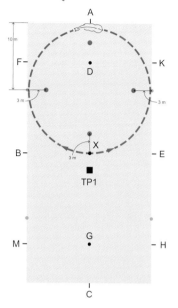

Four cones are required for this exercise. Place each 3m in from the arena wall: one opposite A; a second in line with the circle point between F and B (10m from the short side); a third on the centre line 3m from X; and a fourth in line with the circle point between K and E.

TP1 gives a view of both the inside and outside of horse and rider.

TOP TIP

The four cones also help the rider to regulate the rhythm of the horse's gait. Ask them to count the number of strides the horse takes on each quarter-circle, between the cones. There should be the same number of strides on each.

Establishing correct flexion and bend in preparation for riding a circle.

26. CONES FOR SINGLE LOOPS

Aims of the exercise

Single loops require accuracy, so using cones here helps the rider to focus on the changes of bend required when riding loops.

Step-by-step explanation of the exercise

❑ Starting in medium walk on the left rein, a shallow loop is ridden from F to M, riding around the cone opposite B. A second loop is ridden on the next long side, inclining from the track at H, around the cone opposite E, and returning to the track at K.

❑ The rider changes the rein to repeat the exercise on the right rein.

❑ Once successful in walk, the rider can proceed to trot.

❑ Using the first cone after A as a marker, the rider rides through the corner between A and F. After this they straighten the horse and incline off the track, riding to the left side of the cone opposite B. As they approach this cone, they flex the horse to the right. After riding past this cone, they straighten the horse as they return to the track, flexing it to the left again before the third cone opposite M. After riding the corner between M and A, they straighten the horse, completing the loop.

❑ Using cones to define the shallow loops helps the rider to improve their skills in keeping the horse in balance when inclining off the track.

❑ Sitting trot focuses the rider on accuracy, while rising trot can be useful here for encouraging rhythm and swing through the back while riding the changes of bend required.

Common faults and how to rectify these

• It can be difficult to assess the shape of a shallow loop, and how far to incline off the track. If the loop is too shallow, the rider does not get a feel for

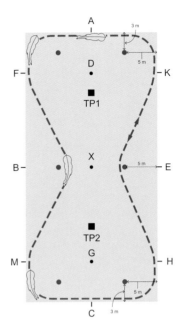

Place three cones on each of the quarter lines, 5m in from the long side arena wall. The corner cones should be 3m in from the wall on the short side. The centre cones are in line with E and B.

From TP1, assess horse and rider at the A end of the arena, and from TP2, assess them at the C end of the arena.

the changes of bend required, so placing the cones on the quarter lines, 5m in from the wall, helps to improve the rider's understanding of the degree of bend and balance required when riding loops. The centre cone of the loop can be moved closer to, or away from, the wall to adjust the amount of incline as may be required by a dressage test.

• The corner cones help the rider to avoid the mistake of cutting the corners, an indication of a lack of body bend in the horse, and the rider leaning in. Bringing the rider's awareness to straightening the horse at A and C helps them to keep their weight central in the saddle, making the changes of flexion in the horse easier to achieve.

27. POLES FOR STRAIGHT LINES

Aims of the exercise

In this exercise, the pairs of poles are used as a checkpoint for the straightness of horse and rider on the long sides of the arena, on the quarter line, 5m in from the wall.

Step-by-step explanation of the exercise

- Starting on the left rein at A in medium walk, horse and rider turn off the track onto the quarter line, riding between the two poles opposite B. They continue on the quarter line before turning left onto the track before C, turning onto the three-quarter line after C (being three-quarters of the way across the arena). Finally, they proceed straight between the poles opposite E, returning to the track before A, from where the exercise can be repeated.

- A change of rein is required to ride this exercise on the right rein, turning onto the quarter line after A, and the three-quarter line after C.

- Once achieved in walk, they can proceed to trot.

- View horse and rider from the side, to assess outline and way of going, and from the front, and rear. View to assess straightness.

- Make sure the rider flexes the horse to the left, in order to turn onto the quarter/three-quarter lines. Check they are positioned equidistant from each pole to ensure accuracy.

- Taking sitting trot between the poles aids the rider's accuracy, and is a useful opportunity to check that the rider is sitting with equal weight on both seat bones, and in both stirrups. Check their hand position is correct, and their rein contact is even. The poles give a guide to assess the straightness of the horse and rider when viewing both from the front and from the rear view.

Common faults and how to rectify these

- Turning onto the quarter and three-quarter lines requires accurate riding. Imbalance, caused by a lack of support from the rider's outside aids, or

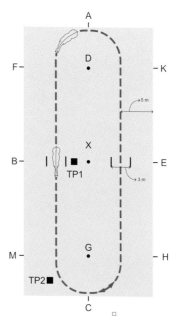

Place two parallel poles 3m apart opposite B, a distance wide enough for the horse to pass through comfortably, while close enough to guide horse and rider on a straight line. The rider rides straight between these, on the quarter line, 5m in from the wall. Place a second pair of poles opposite E.

From TP1 view horse and rider from the side, to assess outline and way of going, and from TP2 assess horse and rider head on to assess straightness.

lack of support from their inside leg, results in crookedness. A crooked turn results in lack of straightness.

- Focusing on riding between the pair of poles helps the rider to gauge their turn accurately, which, in turn, leads to being able to straighten the horse, keeping it parallel to the long sides of the arena.

- From a side view, the ground pole gives an eye-line for assessing the horse's balance and outline, whether it is on its forehand, or taking weight behind. Check the speed of the gait, which impacts on balance.

28. POLES FOR CHANGES OF REIN (DIRECTION) ON THE DIAGONAL

Aims of the exercise

The aim here is to encourage the rider to accurately ride changes of rein on the diagonal lines of the arena.

Step-by-step explanation of the exercise

❑ Starting from A on the left rein in medium walk, horse and rider proceed through the corner between A and F. On reaching F, they change the rein on the diagonal line FH, passing between the parallel poles before X. Riding through the corners between H and C, and C and M, the rider turns the horse onto the diagonal line towards K, passing between the pair of parallel poles before X. On reaching K, they ride through the corner between K and A, to complete the exercise.

❑ Once the exercise is achieved in walk, horse and rider can repeat it in trot.

❑ Assess the accuracy of riding through the corners: view the turn from F onto the diagonal line, and the turn away from the diagonal line at H, tracking right. Similarly, assess the turn onto the other diagonal line at M, and away, tracking left at K.

❑ The placing of the poles on the diagonal lines ensures horse and rider pass exactly over X, the centre point of the arena.

❑ Observe how straight the rider keeps the horse on the diagonal line, and the accuracy of their placement of the horse between the poles. Ensure the rider pays attention to riding accurately through the corners, preparing the horse for each turn by flexing it in the direction of travel. Look for straightness over X, also assessing the balance and outline of the horse, and the quality of the walk, namely rhythm and length of stride.

Common faults and how to rectify these

• When riding this exercise in trot, a common error is for the rider to cut the corners, turning

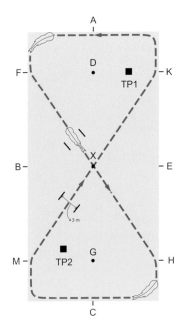

Place two pairs of parallel poles, 3m apart, on the diagonal lines from F to H, and from M to K, so that horse and rider pass through them before X on the respective diagonals. From TP1, view the turn from F onto the diagonal line, and from TP2, assess the turn onto the diagonal from M to K, looking for how the rider straightens the horse between the poles.

too soon. This unbalances the horse, making it difficult for the rider to accurately ride onto the diagonal line. The poles are useful here as a correction, giving the rider a point of focus to aim towards, helping them to straighten the horse before X.

• Lack of preparation for the turns onto, and away from, the diagonal lines runs the risk of leaving the track too late. Make sure the rider uses their outside rein to control the bend in the horse's neck, and to prevent drifting to the outside, and use their outside leg, behind the girth, to bring the horse off the track, and onto the diagonal, turning their body accordingly.

29. POLES FOR FIGURES OF EIGHT

Aims of the exercise

This exercise is to clarify the accuracy of the change of bend required when changing direction at the centre point of the figure of eight.

Step-by-step explanation of the exercise

Starting from X, between the poles on the left rein in medium walk, facing E, horse and rider proceed onto a 20m-diameter circle left. On returning to X, a 20m-diameter circle right is ridden, to complete a figure of eight.

❏ The exercise can be ridden in the opposite direction by starting on the right rein at X, facing B.

❏ Once achieved in walk, it can be ridden in trot.

❏ On reaching X, the halfway point of the circle, the rider straightens the horse for a horse's length (3–4 strides), passing between the poles. They then flex the horse to the right to prepare for the 20m-diameter circle to the right, at the C end of the arena. On returning to X, they straighten the horse for 3–4 strides between the poles, before flexing it to the left, completing the 20m-diameter circle at the A end of the arena.

❏ View the symmetry of both circles, checking the rider flexes the horse to the left for the circle ridden on the left rein, and to the right for the circle on the right rein, to ensure the horse is prepared for each in turn.

❏ When riding the figure of eight in rising trot, ask the rider to change their diagonal between the poles.

❏ Assess the straightness of horse and rider at the tangent where both circles meet, making sure the horse is balanced before proceeding in the new direction.

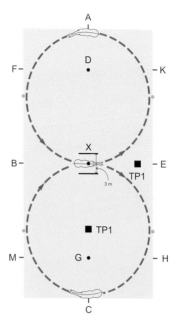

Lay a pair of parallel poles either side of X, 3m apart, across the centre line between B and E. From TP1, assess the straightness of horse and rider at the tangent where both circles meet. TP2 gives a view of the whole figure of eight, rotating as needed.

• Check that both the circles are ridden the same size and shape, reaching both the circle points and the centre point of each short side of the arena at A and C respectively. Riders often find turning in one direction easier than the other, so check they ride the horse with consistency throughout the figure of eight.

• To ensure accuracy in changing direction over X in trot, ask the rider to ride a few strides of sitting trot between the poles.

Common faults and how to rectify these

• Should the rider find the changes of flexion before and after X difficult, ask them to halt the horse between the poles. This defines the straightness of the horse required between flexion left and flexion right. It offers you the opportunity to coach the rider in the halt, making sure they understand flexion and bend, and to check their position and aids.

TOP TIP

To improve the horse's balance when riding this exercise in trot, ask the rider to ride a horse's length (3–4 strides) in walk between the poles. This also gives them thinking time to apply the changes of flexion required.

30. COMBINATION PROPS FOR ACCURACY

Aims of the exercise

The aim here is to put together prior learning, test-ing the rider's ability to ride turns and straight lines accurately, preparing the horse for each required movement.

Step-by-step explanation of the exercise

❑ Starting from K on the left rein in medium walk, horse and rider proceed onto the centre line at A, by riding a half 10m-diameter circle, using the cone to guide them. They proceed on the centre line, passing between the parallel poles before X. After riding through the poles, they incline straight back to the track at the circle point before H. On reaching the track at H, they track right.

❑ Horse and rider then turn onto the centre line at C, by riding a half 10m-diameter circle from H, around the cone. On the centre line, they pass between the parallel poles before X. They then incline straight back to the track at the circle point before K. On reaching the track, they proceed on the left rein. The exercise can then be repeated.

❑ Once achieved in walk, the exercise can be ridden in trot.

❑ To ensure the rider maintains the horse's balance throughout this exercise, transitions can be included. When riding the exercise in walk, ask the rider to halt each time they pass between the poles. This also gives the opportunity for suggesting any necessary corrections to improve the horse's way of going.

❑ When riding the exercise in trot, walking one horse's length between the poles gives an opportunity to check if the horse is working correctly through its back. Look for fluency in the transitions, the horse's outline and the quality of the contact with the bit.

Common faults and how to rectify these

• Over-shooting the centre line is a common problem, which can be avoided by the rider taking time to flex the horse correctly in preparation.

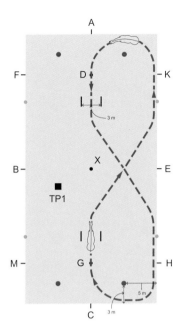

Place two pairs of parallel poles, 3m apart, on the centre line. The first pair are laid in line with the circle point between K and E, 10m from the short side of the arena. The second pair are in line with the circle point between E and H. Place one cone in each corner of the arena. They should be 5m in from the long side wall, on the quarter lines, and 3m in from the wall on the short side. View the whole exercise from TP1, moving as needed.

Check they are supporting the horse with their outside aids, and not using too much inside rein when turning.

• When riding an incline back to the track, the rider may allow the horse to drift sideways. Make sure there is a clear definition between them turning in the direction of travel, and straightening the horse as they ride towards the designated circle point.

TOP TIP

Halting on the centre line, between the poles, is good preparation for riding dressage tests.

INTERMEDIATE DRESSAGE (20 × 60m ARENA)

31. STRETCHING

Aims of the exercise

When stretching the horse, the rider should be encouraged to ride the horse on a long rein, enabling it to loosen up through its back.

Step-by-step explanation of the exercise

Starting from A on the left rein in medium walk, horse and rider follow the line of a 20m-diameter half-circle. On reaching P, they turn onto the diagonal line PS. On reaching S, they commence a 20m-diameter half-circle right before riding straight on the diagonal line RV. They then ride a 20m-diameter half-circle at the A end of the arena.

❑ This pattern can be repeated as required.

❑ This exercise can be ridden in working trot and canter, changing leg through trot on the short diagonals.

❑ On the half-circles at each end of the arena, look for the rider encouraging the horse to bend correctly through its body. Look for how the rider straightens the horse on the short diagonals.

❑ Make sure the rider keeps their hands low and wide, easing the reins through their fingers. This keeps the horse in balance, while encouraging it to stretch forwards and downwards into the contact. The rider can take the reins shorter as required, without changing their upper body position.

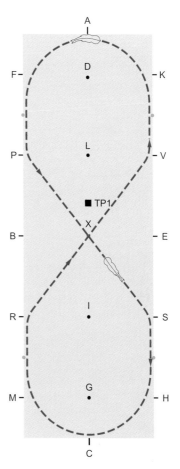

TP1 gives a view of the whole arena, rotating as required.

Common faults and how to rectify these

• If the horse is tense at the beginning of this exercise, instruct the rider to maintain the contact with the bit to guide the horse into a longer, lower outline. Should the rider have the reins too long at this point, there is a risk of the horse spooking, so it is safer for the rider to keep the horse between hand and leg until they reach a point of relaxation, where the reins can be lengthened. Once the horse lowers its neck it will relax through its back, and the rider will be able to proceed to trot and canter work on a long rein.

• When working in a long, low outline, the rider often collapses their upper body, losing core strength. However, riding this exercise in a light, forwards, seat is of great benefit for the freedom of the horse's back, and develops the rider's balance.

• Once the horse is relaxed, the hands can be brought closer together, either side of the pommel of the saddle, to bring the horse on the bit, working in an outline appropriate for its level of training.

> ## TOP TIP
>
> This stretching exercise can, and should be, ridden at frequent intervals during schooling and can be interspersed in any exercise to promote relaxation, both mentally and physically. It can also be used as a cool-down exercise.

32. TRANSITIONS

Aims of the exercise

The aim here is to improve accuracy when riding both upward and downward transitions.

Step-by-step explanation of the exercise

Starting from A on the left rein, horse and rider proceed in medium walk for a horse's length at A. To follow, a transition to working trot sitting is ridden. They then proceed around the arena, walking for a horse's length at B, C, and E (shown in green). A change of rein is ridden down the centre line, walking for a horse's length at X (shown in green).

❏ Have in your mind's eye the 3–4 strides required to ride one horse's length, so you can help the rider to accurately place the horse at each letter, A, B, C, E and X. Look for correct application of the aids, paying attention to the bracing of the rider's back in each of the downward transitions. Encourage the rider to prepare for each transition into medium walk by using half-halts to keep the horse in balance, with weight on its haunches.

❏ When riding the upward transitions into trot, a half-halt is also required as preparation, to maintain balance. Look for the suppleness of the rider's back as they absorb the spring of the working trot transition. If the rider has difficulty keeping their seat, ask them to slow the tempo of the walk and trot, to give them time to feel the movement of the horse's back more clearly. Once established, the tempo can be increased.

Common faults and how to rectify these

• When focusing on riding the transitions at the designated letters, the rider may lose focus on riding through the corners accurately, which can in turn affect the horse's balance and straightness on the long sides. If this happens, *refer to Exercise 5: Corners.*

• Look for the consistency of the medium walk for each horse's length. Often, riders have difficulty on picking up the rhythm of the walk, either hurrying, leading to the horse running into trot, or going too slowly, losing impulsion. Keeping the medium walk active and purposeful ensures the horse has sufficient energy for the transitions into, and out of, working trot.

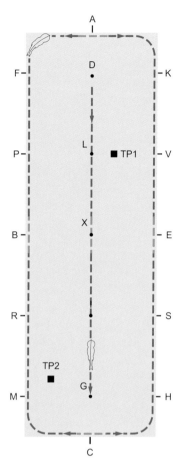

TP1 gives a view of the A end of the arena and the centre line, with TP2 giving a view of the C end.

• The horse's outline should be consistent throughout this exercise. Ensure the optimum length of rein to keep the horse on the bit is maintained by the rider, noticing their co-ordination of rein, seat and leg aids. Particular attention should be paid to their use of their hands in the transitions, how they close their fingers, and remain supple in their wrists.

TOP TIP

This exercise can be progressed by riding it in canter, trotting for a horse's length at each of the specified letters. A change of leg through trot can be ridden on the centre line over X.

33. MEDIUM TROT

Aims of the exercise

The aim here is to develop medium strides in trot by developing transitions between working and medium trot.

Step-by-step explanation of the exercise

Starting from A on the left rein, in working trot, horse and rider proceed on the track to P.

❏ They then change the rein from P to S in medium trot (shown in green), riding a transition back into working trot at S. Continuing in collected trot to R, a change of rein is ridden in medium trot RV (shown in green). Working trot is resumed at V.

❏ The exercise can then be repeated.

❏ On riding this exercise, make sure the rider flexes the horse accurately through the corners at the beginning of the diagonals, using half-halts. This prepares the horse for medium trot by developing the carrying power, and engagement, of the hind legs.

❏ The horse should be absolutely straight in the diagonal, and push from both hind legs with equal effort as the rider asks for medium trot. The reins should be eased to allow the horse to lengthen its neck as it lengthens its strides.

❏ On returning to the track at the end of the diagonals, make sure they establish flexion and bend as they return to the track, Also, the horse's frame should be shortened, using half-halts, as the rider brings the horse back to working trot.

❏ The medium trot can be ridden either sitting or rising. Rising trot can help to develop the length of stride, and is useful if the rider's seat is not yet developed sufficiently to sit to medium trot without hindering the horse's back movement. However, sitting to the trot is the aim, as the rider has more influence on the quality of the gait using their seat.

Common faults and how to rectify these

• In order to lengthen the trot stride, as required with medium trot, a common mistake is to ride faster. This has the opposite effect of shortening the stride, with a hurried tempo, rather than maintaining the trot rhythm and developing the pushing power of the hind-quarters to generate impulsion.

• To rectify this, ask the rider to use half-halts to bring the working trot towards collection, ensuring the forehand is light without relying

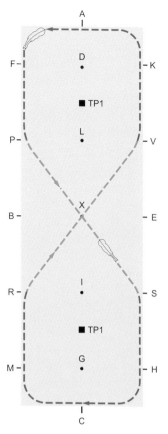

TP1 gives a view of the transitions between collected and medium trot at the A end of the arena, and TP2 at the C end.

on the reins to bring the horse into a rounder outline, with lowering of the haunches. Once the horse responds to the rider's aids, and the trot becomes more elevated, they can ride a progressive transition to medium trot.

• With a progressive transition, the risk of the horse running forwards is reduced. The rider needs to keep the horse between hand and leg, co-ordinating the movement of their back and hips to generate the required lengthened strides of medium trot.

Straightness is important for maintaining balance in medium trot.

34. CHANGES OF REIN (ACROSS THE ARENA)

Aims of the exercise

This exercise tests the rider's accuracy when turning across the arena to change the rein over the centre line.

Step-by-step explanation of the exercise

Starting on the left rein from A in medium walk, the rider changes the rein across the arena from P to V, and proceeds on the right rein on the long side from V to S. A second change of rein is ridden across the arena from S to R, proceeding on the left rein to C, before continuing around the track back to A.

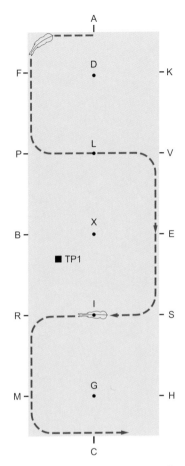

TP1 gives a view of both changes of rein.

- ❏ The exercise can then be repeated. Alternatively, the exercise can be ridden in mirror-image by starting on the right rein at A.
- ❏ When riding the changes of rein, make sure the rider turns the horse by riding a quarter 10m-diameter circle, in the same way as riding corners (*see* Exercise 5: Corners). The lines across the centre line, connecting the turns, should be straight, and parallel to the short sides of the arena.
- ❏ Check the rider's ability to change the horse's flexion and bend, and ensure they ride straight as they cross the centre line.
- ❏ With changes of direction in quick succession, such as in this exercise, remind the rider to use half-halts to keep the horse balanced, and check they are consistent in their aids and position in both directions.
- ❏ Once achieved in walk, this exercise can be ridden in trot.

Common faults and how to rectify these

- • Cutting the corners can be caused by the rider leaning in, or relying on the inside rein to turn the horse, rather than using their body and leg aids. Correct the rider's balance in the saddle and the use of their outside leg to ask the horse to turn, and their inside leg to support the horse. Make sure they maintain a consistent contact with the outside rein to control the amount of neck bend.
- • Drifting out on corners can result from a lack of body bend in the horse, requiring more support from the rider's outside leg. Check the rider's inside

leg remains by the girth. If is brought too far back, this can push the horse's hind-quarters out.

- • A lack of straightness across the centre line can result in a lack of definition between the horse's flexion and bend to the left and right. The rider will not have time to prepare the horse to turn on the new direction.

TOP TIP

Transitions can be added to the change of rein. For example, when riding the exercise in working trot, one horse's length in walk could be ridden over the centre line before proceeding again in trot.

35. CIRCLES (15m DIAMETER)

Aims of the exercise

The aim here is to assist the rider in adapting the flexion and bend of the horse when riding 15m-diameter circles (as opposed to 20m-diameter circles).

Step-by-step explanation of the exercise

Starting from A on the left rein in working trot, the rider proceeds around the arena to P, where they ride a 15m-diameter circle. On returning to the track, they continue in trot to S, where a second 15m-diameter circle is ridden (shown in green). They continue in working trot around the arena to A, from where the exercise can be repeated.

❏ After a change of rein, the circles can be ridden to the right.

❏ Use the corners of the arena to assess the bend of the horse, and the rider's position and aiding as preparation for the circles. Look for consistency in the shape and size of the circles, checking the rider commences, and finishes, each circle exactly at the designated letter. The rhythm of the trot should be regular, with an even length of stride. This should not alter as the rider brings the horse onto the circles from the track, and returns to the track afterwards. Once achieved in trot, this exercise can be ridden in working canter.

Common faults and how to rectify these

• The rider's balance affects the ability of the horse to follow the line of the circles. Leaning in draws the horse inwards, causing a tendency to fall in on the inside shoulder. As a consequence of this, the haunches may swing to the outside, so the horse is no longer 'straight', that is, with the hind legs following in the tracks of the front legs. To rectify this, ensure the rider maintains correct weight distribution across their seat-bones and into their stirrups. This applies to riding the circles in walk, trot and canter.

• Should there be a lack of flexion, or the horse is incorrectly flexed to the outside on the circles, a useful exercise is to ask the rider to use counter flexion/true flexion on the long sides of the arena

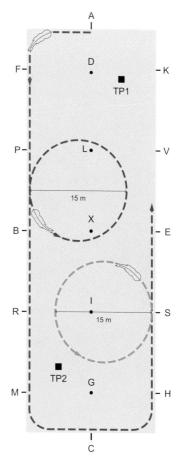

TP1 gives a view of the A end of the arena, and TP2 the C end.

to create more suppleness through the horse's poll. This also has the effect of relaxing the jaw, and developing an even contact with the bit. Once this is established, the circles should be ridden again.

TOP TIP

Variations within the gait can be added, by riding in working trot on the track and medium trot on the circles. Alternatively, working canter can be ridden on the track with medium canter ridden on the circles.

36. SHOULDER-IN

Aims of the exercise

Shoulder-in is a great exercise for improving the rider's understanding of collection, flexion and bend, and positioning the horse in lateral work such as leg-yield.

Step-by-step explanation of the exercise

Starting from A on the left rein in collected walk, the rider proceeds on the track to P, maintaining left flexion through the corner between A and F. On reaching P, the rider commences shoulder-in, bringing the horse's forehand off the track to the required angle of 30 degrees (working on three tracks). The horse is ridden straight after R, with the shoulder-in being repeated on the next long side between S and V. The horse is then ridden straight on the track to A to conclude the exercise.

❑ A change to the rein is required to ride shoulder-in on the right rein.

❑ Once achieved in walk, this exercise can be ridden in trot.

❑ In this exercise, riding the preceding corners correctly establishes the correct flexion and bend of the horse required for shoulder-in. Encourage the rider to be mindful of their position and aids before commencing shoulder-in on the long sides.

❑ On the first long side, as they bring the horse's shoulders off the track at P, make sure their outside rein and leg support the outside of the horse. Check the position of their inside leg by the girth, as they ask the horse to step forwards and sideways on the track.

❑ Also, evaluate how the rider ends the shoulder-in, by bringing the horse's shoulders back onto the track at R. They should maintain flexion, though, in preparation for the following corner between M and C. These observations should be repeated as the rider commences shoulder-in at S, and finishes the movement at V.

❑ When performing this exercise in trot, working trot can be ridden on the short sides of the arena, collecting the trot for the shoulder-in.

Common faults and how to rectify these

• Attempting shoulder-in with a lack of body bend in the horse results in moving sideways along the track on four tracks (as in leg yield), not three tracks. Ask the rider to create more bend, using their inside leg, and look for the horse's inside hind and outside fore being on the same track.

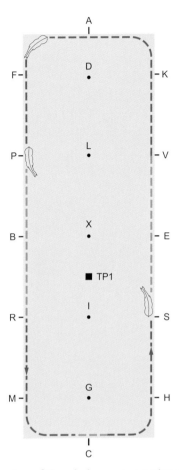

TP1 gives a view of the whole arena, rotating as needed.

• If the horse has too much neck bend, as a result of the rider using their inside rein too strongly, address the support issue with their outside rein. This is necessary to bring the horse's shoulders off the track.

• The haunches may swing out as a result of the rider bringing their inside leg back when asking for shoulder-in. Make sure the rider's inside leg remains at the girth.

TOP TIP

Always rectify issues with shoulder-in in collected walk, to give the rider time to correct their technique, and the horse time to understand what is required.

Riding shoulder-in.

37. LOOPS (DOUBLE)

Aims of the exercise

Riding double loops on the long sides of the arena improves the horse's suppleness, and the rider's co-ordination of the aids.

Step-by-step explanation of the exercise

Starting from A on the left rein in medium walk, the rider rides through the corner between A and F, bringing the horse off the track at F, inclining 3m, before returning to the track at B. From B, they incline 3m a second time, returning to the track at M, forming a double loop on the long side. The exercise can be repeated on the next long side between H and F.

❏ A change of rein is required to repeat the double loops on the right rein.

❏ Once successful in medium walk, the rider can proceed to working trot. The loops can also be ridden in counter-canter.

❏ As the corner between A and F is ridden, assess the positioning of the horse to the left. On bringing the horse off the track at F, the rider should straighten the horse for a few steps before reaching the deepest part of the loop, opposite P.

❏ At this point, the horse is bent to the right, returning to the track at B. Look for accuracy here, as a change of bend to the left is ridden, in preparation for riding the second loop. Again, the rider should straighten the horse before bending it to the right, returning to the track at M. Left position (flexion) should be maintained to ride accurately through the corner between M and C. Both loops should be ridden the same depth off the track.

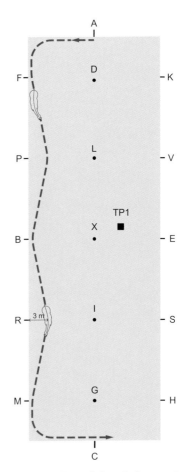

TP1 gives a view of the whole exercise.

Common faults and how to rectify these

• This exercise requires balance, so the rider should use frequent half-halts to develop the engagement of the hind-quarters. This lightens the forehand, making it easier for the rider to turn the horse as required.

• If changes of bend are not clearly indicated to the horse, uneven loops can result, with the horse drifting off line. In this case, address the rider's use of their weight aids through their seat. Focusing on the rider sitting equally on both seat bones on the straight steps, between the changes of bend, helps to address any tendency to sit too much to one side.

• Putting too much weight on the inside seat bone when asking for bend causes the horse to put too much weight on its inside foreleg, and displaces the haunches to the outside. Sitting too much to the outside causes the horse to load its outside hind leg, causing difficulty in turning. Ask the rider to be aware of keeping weight on both seat bones to correct this. Any difference in weight on the seat bones should be subtle.

> ## TOP TIP
>
> The rider should adjust the tempo of the walk, or trot, to maintain balance throughout this exercise. This exercise is useful in improving the technique of counter-canter.

38. SERPENTINES (THREE LOOPS)

Aims of the exercise

The aim here is to improve the horse's balance and flexibility with the changes of direction involved. Balance and accuracy is required when distinguishing between the curved loops and the straight lines across the centre line.

Step-by-step explanation of the exercise

Starting from A on the left rein, in medium walk, the rider commences a three-loop serpentine, describing three 20m-diameter loops, crossing the centre line twice, with the centre point of the second (middle) loop reaching the track at E.

❏ A change of rein is required to ride the serpentine commencing on the right rein from A.

❏ This exercise can be ridden in working trot, and in working canter, with a change of lead, through trot, across the centre line.

❏ Make sure the rider is aware that the serpentine starts at A by riding the horse onto the first 20m-diameter loop, as though commencing a circle. On reaching the quarter line, they should straighten the horse in preparation for crossing the centre line.

❏ On reaching the three-quarter line, they should flex the horse to the right in order to commence the second loop. After the second loop, they need to straighten the horse on this quarter line, flexing the horse to the left as they reach the three-quarter line as they commence the third, and last, loop.

❏ The serpentine finishes by horse and rider following the curved line of the loop to its end point at C.

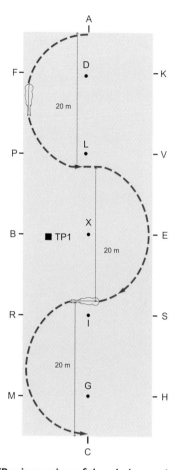

TP1 gives a view of the whole exercise.

Common faults and how to rectify these

• A common mistake is to ride uneven loops, by riding into the corner between A and F. To be accurate, the serpentine begins at A, so the first loop starts at A. The corner should not be ridden, as this detracts from the curved line of the first serpentine loop.

• Similarly, if the rider rides into the corner as the serpentine ends, between M and C, the last loop of the serpentine will lose its rounded shape. This helps the rider to distinguish between the corners and the serpentine loops by explaining the difference.

• A lack of straightness over the centre line indicates imbalance in the rider's seat, leaning in one direction or the other, impacting on the horse's

balance. Make sure the rider rides accurately across the centre line after completing the first loop, and keeps the horse in balance as they commence the second loop.

• Assess the rider's weight aids as they ride across the centre line for the second time, and proceed to the third loop.

• Should the horse's hind-quarters swing out on the loops, this is indicative of a lack of preparation by the rider for flexing the horse in the direction of travel, and straightening across the centre line each time.

TOP TIP

This exercise can also be ridden in canter without changes of lead, to develop counter-canter.

39. LEG YIELD

Aims of the exercise

Leg yield introduces horse and rider to moving the horse forwards and sideways across the arena.

Step-by-step explanation of the exercise

Starting on the left rein, the rider turns onto the centre line from A in collected walk, commencing shoulder-fore at D. From L, they ride leg yield from L to R. On reaching the track at R, they proceed in shoulder-in to M. The horse is ridden straight on the next long side before repeating the exercise.

❑ A change of rein is required to ride the exercise on the right rein.

❑ Make sure the rider turns the horse accurately onto the centre line, as this will prepare them for the shoulder-fore between D to L. At L, to commence leg yield towards R, they increase the pressure with their inside leg, as the driving aid, asking the horse to step forwards and sideways, maintaining left flexion, on the diagonal line to R. Riding shoulder-in fluidly from the leg yield, on reaching the track at R, is a test of correctly applied aids.

❑ It can be helpful to remind the rider that the inside aids are on the inside of the bend of the horse, and the outside aids are on the outside of the bend of the horse. Focusing on keeping the horse's ears level is a guide to avoiding any tipping of the horse's head.

❑ The rider's inside leg, which should always be nearer to the girth than the outside leg, is the dominant aid when asking for leg yield. Their outside leg plays a passive, supportive role, controlling the amount of travel in a sideways direction.

Common faults and how to rectify these

• Riders often ask the horse to travel sideways by bringing their inside leg back. Viewing leg-yield as riding shoulder-fore on a diagonal line ensures the rider maintains correct flexion, with the horse moving away from their inside leg.

• A common mistake is to allow the horse to drift back to the track at the end of a leg yield, rather than maintaining support with the outside rein and leg. Reaching the track after the leg yield in

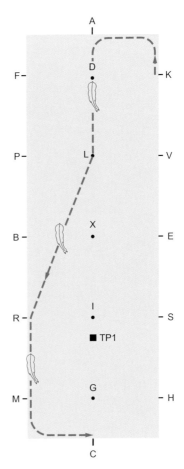

TP1 gives a view of the whole exercise, rotating as needed.

shoulder-in is a test of a correct inside flexion and bend.

• Make sure the inside rein is not used too strongly in an effort to maintain flexion away from the direction of travel. If the leg yield is ridden correctly, the rider should be able to give the rein, with the inside hand moving forwards, without the horse losing balance.

TOP TIP

When riding leg yield, it is of benefit to the rider if they have an understanding of shoulder-in (Exercise 36. Leg yield is ridden with less body bend than shoulder-in.

40. TURN AROUND THE FOREHAND

Aims of the exercise

This exercise develops the horse's understanding of moving away from the rider's inside leg pressure into the supportive outside rein.

Step-by-step explanation of the exercise

The rider commences a three-loop serpentine from A in medium walk. On crossing the centre line each time, they collect the walk, and ride a turn around the forehand to the left, before reaching the track. They return across the centre line after the turn around the forehand, riding another serpentine loop on the long side between F and M.

❑ Riding this exercise, as half-serpentine loops, horse and rider stay on the left rein throughout, enabling the rider to focus on left flexion and bend. As the rider executes the first serpentine loop, make sure that the rhythm and tempo of the horse's medium walk is maintained, in order to keep it relaxed and listening to the rider's aids.

❑ On reaching the quarter line, ask them to collect the walk, increasing the engagement of the horse's hind-quarters in preparation for the first turn around the forehand on the three-quarter line. On completing this, they ride forwards in collected walk, riding the second serpentine loop, with its deepest point reaching the track at B.

❑ Check the flexion and bend of the horse, and the rider's weight aids. They return across the centre line for a second time, executing a second turn around the forehand on the three-quarter line opposite S. Make sure there is sufficient engagement of the horse's hind-quarters before each turn around the forehand.

Common faults and how to rectify these

• Riders often bring their inside leg back to ask the horse to turn. This may work, but will bring confusion when learning turn-on-the-haunches and half-pirouettes. Using shoulder-fore as preparation ensures the rider keeps their inside leg by the girth, and their outside leg behind when riding turn on the forehand.

• If the horse travels too far as it moves away from the rider's inside leg aid, ask the rider to halt before asking the horse to turn in order to keep

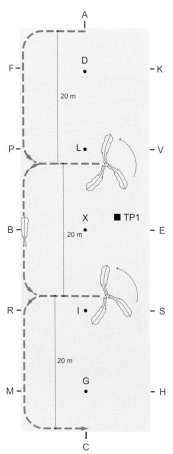

TP1 gives a view of the whole exercise, moving as needed.

the horse on their aids, particularly maintaining control of the turn with the outside rein and leg.

• Loss of flexion and bend can cause disruption to the turn around the forehand, so address this as the rider rides the serpentine, where there is time and opportunity to do so before riding the next turn around the forehand. Turn around the forehand (from collected walk)/turn on the forehand (from halt).

TOP TIP

A turn *on* the forehand is ridden from halt, executed with the horse's front legs marking time on the spot, whereas a turn *around* the forehand is ridden in collected walk, with the forelegs stepping sideways, without crossing, describing a small half-circle.

INTERMEDIATE JUMPING (20 × 60m ARENA)

41. REFINING JUMPING POSITION

Aims of the exercise

Improving the rider's balance in jumping position with the aim of an independent rein contact. The rider should not be reliant on the rein contact to keep their balance.

Step-by-step explanation of the exercise

❏ Commencing between A and F on the left rein in rising trot, the rider proceeds on the track to P. At P a 20m-diameter circle left is ridden (shown in green). On the circle, the rider gives the inside hand forwards on the first half of the circle from P to V, and the outside hand on the second half of the circle, from V to P.

❏ They proceed straight on the track to R, riding half a 20m-diameter circle to S. On this half-circle, they give both hands forwards. From S, they proceed straight on the track, keeping the contact with both hands. On reaching the trotting poles at A, both hands are given forwards on riding over the poles.

❏ A change of rein is required to ride this exercise on the right rein.

❏ As horse and rider proceed around the circle, the inside hand is moved forwards far enough to release the contact with the bit, while maintaining contact with the outside rein. The reason for this is to test the effectiveness of the rider's aids when turning the horse, without over-reliance on the inside rein. Giving the outside rein tests the rider's balance, and their ability to keep the horse on the circle line without over-reliance on the outside rein.

❏ Giving both hands forwards on the 20m-diameter half-circle, from R to S, releasing the contact, confirms the rider's independent seat, that is being able to control and remain in balance with the horse, without relying on the reins.

❏ Giving both reins forwards, when trotting over the poles at A, allows the horse freedom through its neck when more animated in its gait. This also tests independence of the rider's seat, which will later be necessary when jumping.

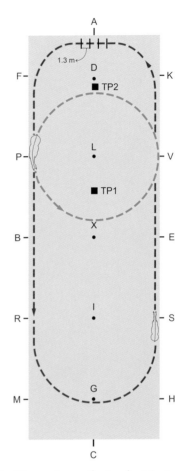

Set four trotting poles on the track at A at 1.3m apart.

TP1 gives a view of the exercise, rotating as necessary. Being close enough to the trotting poles to watch the rider in detail can be viewed from TP2.

Common faults and how to rectify these

• A common mistake that riders make when 'giving with the hands' is to lean forwards with the body, rather than moving the arms. The rider should maintain their upper body position, so as not to disturb the horse's balance when releasing the contact.

• To improve their balance, the rider can alternate rising trot with a light forward seat. Giving both hands forwards simultaneously, releasing the contact, tests the security of their position, while allowing the horse freedom of its neck. This is good preparation for giving the hands forwards over a fence.

42. WARM-UP

Aims of the exercise

The aim is to loosen the horse up in trot and canter, allowing the horse to stretch forwards and downwards, stretching through its back in preparation for jumping.

Step-by-step explanation of the exercise

❑ Starting from A on the left rein on a half 20m-diameter circle in working trot, the rider rides a transition to working canter left between B and R, riding a half-circle from R to S (shown in green), passing between the jump wings.

❑ At S, they ride a transition to trot. They ask for left lead canter at V, riding a half 20m-diameter circle from V to P (shown in green), passing between the jump wings, with a transition back into trot at P. They then ask for left lead canter at R, proceeding around the school. A half 20m-diameter circle is ridden at the C end, from M to H, before returning to A to repeat the exercise.

❑ A change of rein is required to ride this exercise on the right rein, with right lead canter on the half circles.

❑ Transitions between trot and canter are beneficial to loosening up the horse's back muscles, particularly for jumping. This is because of the difference in how the horse uses its back in trot, with the leg sequence being in diagonal pairs, and in canter, being a unilateral gait, differentiating between right and left canter.

❑ This exercise helps the rider to learn, by feel, the optimum timing of when to ask for each transition by the half circles in canter: the upwards transition is asked for coming off the track, and the downward transition on returning to the track.

Common faults and how to rectify these

• Because this exercise is aimed at preparation for jumping, riding through the pairs of wings helps the rider to focus on where they are going as well as the transitions into, and out of, canter.

• Ensure the rider keeps a steady rhythm throughout this exercise, as too much speed causes the horse to be unbalanced, and affects the precision of the transitions.

• As the focus here is on warming up both horse and rider, that is loosening up the muscles, and developing a relaxed frame of mind, the rider

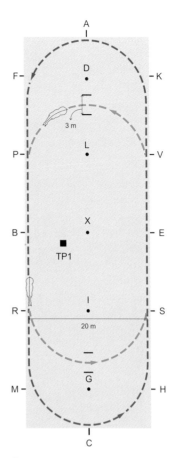

Set a pair of jump wings, 3m apart, on the centre line between D and L. Place a second pair on the centre line between I and G.

From TP1, rotate to view horse and rider passing through both sets of poles.

should use their seat and rein contact to maintain the outline of the horse. The rider should not restrict the horse's ability to lengthen and lower its neck into the contact, as this will impact on the quality of the transitions.

• If horse and rider overshoot the point at which a transition should be made, they should be allowed to continue in trot, or canter, until the right moment presents itself. Check their transition preparation is sound, and help them to feel for the timing of each transition.

TOP TIP

The quality of the transitions is paramount in establishing harmony between horse and rider, essential for successful jumping.

43. PERFECTING LINES OF APPROACH

Aims of the exercise

The aim here is to establish changes of direction, with a straight approach to each fence.

Step-by-step explanation of the exercise

Set two small fences on the centre line at a distance of 10m either side of X. Construct both 0.8m in height, jumpable in both directions.

❑ Starting from the A end of the arena, in working canter on the left rein, a three-loop serpentine is ridden, with equal loops, jumping each of the fences. A change of canter lead through trot is required after jumping each fence.

❑ After jumping the fence between L and X, a 20m-diameter circle can be added around X (shown in green), giving the rider the opportunity to jump both fences on the right rein to consolidate the lines of approach. They can then change the canter lead through trot, after the fence between I and X, to complete the third serpentine loop.

❑ A change of rein is required to ride the serpentine, starting on the right rein. The circle around X will be ridden to the left.

❑ This exercise requires the rider to plan their approach, riding straight to each fence. The timing of the change of canter lead after each fence affects the change of direction on landing.

❑ When riding the circle around X, assess the quality of the working canter for jumping. The rider should ensure the horse has sufficient engagement so it can take the fences in its stride. The horse should not be hurried, nor be lacking in forwardness, and should jump without any loss of rhythm or balance.

Common faults and how to rectify these

• Hesitation on the approach to a fence runs the risk that the horse may refuse the fence, or run out. To make sure this does not happen, work on the rider's concentration. The rider should focus on a straight approach until the take-off point. Once the horse has landed, they ask for a trot transition, followed by flexing the horse in the required direction.

• If horse and rider have difficulty with alternately changing canter lead when riding the serpentine, they can use the centre circle to practise riding a few

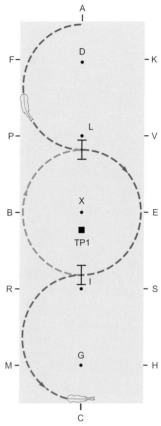

Set a small fence, 0.8m in height, on the centre line at L, and a second at I. Construct both so they can be jumped in both directions.

TP1 gives a clear view of the lines of approach, rotating as required.

trot strides after each fence, without changing lead. Once this is established, they can resume riding the serpentine, changing direction and canter lead.

• Make sure the loops, ridden between the fences, are accurate. Should the horse fall in, or drift out, its balance will be affected, and it may knock the fence. To rectify this, it is important the rider is mindful of their balance between the fences, and of keeping even weight in their stirrups on take-off and landing.

TOP TIP

It is helpful if the rider is proficient with Exercise 38: Serpentines before attempting this exercise. Exercises 13–15: Approach; Take-Off; and Landing; are also useful references.

A secure position in the saddle is essential when riding cross country.
Photo courtesy of Maisie Morgan Eventing.

44. TROTTING POLES WITH A SINGLE FENCE

Aims of the exercise

The aim of this exercise is to establish rhythm when jumping from trot.

Step-by-step explanation of the exercise

This distance between the poles and the jump gives space for the horse to take off over this small fence after trotting over the poles.

- ❏ Starting from A on the left rein, horse and rider proceed in trot around the arena. A 15-, or 20m-, diameter circle is ridden at C (shown in green). The trotting poles and fence are approached on the diagonal line, from S to P.
- ❏ After jumping the fence, horse and rider proceed in canter (right lead) on the diagonal line, with a transition back to trot at F, tracking right.
- ❏ The exercise can be repeated by changing the rein from K to M.
- ❏ To ride this exercise on the right rein, set the poles and jump on the other diagonal line, approaching from M to K.
- ❏ This exercise can be viewed from TP1.
- ❏ Approaching in trot gives the rider time to focus on their line of approach, lining the horse up with the centre of each trotting pole in preparation for the jump.
- ❏ Before the first ground pole, the rider should sit to the trot, in order to feel the movement of the horse's back as it steps over the poles, and takes off over the fence.
- ❏ Focus on their straightness on the long side, and the speed and rhythm of the trot. Ask them to ride an accurate turn through the corner at H onto the diagonal approach line to the fence, taking care that the rider keeps the horse balanced through the turn.

Common faults and how to rectify these

- A common error is to cut the corner at H on the approach. This will make it difficult to present the horse to the centre of the poles. In this instance, it can be helpful to work on turning the horse on a 15m-diameter circle at C before resuming the approach to the fence.
- If the horse rushes towards the poles in trot, or breaks into canter, ask the rider to turn onto the circle, to work on establishing a steady tempo

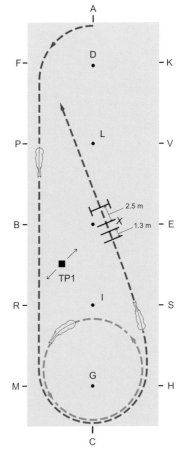

On the diagonal line from S to P, lay three ground poles at a distance of 1.3m from each other. After these, place a jump 0.3m in height at a distance of 2.5m from the poles.

From TP1, rotate to view horse and rider both on the long side and on the diagonal line as they approach the poles.

in working trot, before attempting the approach again. Alternatively, the rider can ride a few steps of walk on the line of approach, after H, before trotting to the poles, which 'checks the brakes'.

- Should the horse rush away after the fence, riding a transition to walk before reaching F gives the rider the opportunity to regain control. Make sure they keep the horse straight, on the diagonal line approaching F.

TOP TIP

Refer to Exercises 13–15: Approach; Take-Off; and Landing.

45. TROTTING POLES WITH A DOUBLE FENCE

Aims of the exercise

Trotting poles before a double help the rider to regulate the horse's speed, maintaining a steady tempo, when approaching the fences.

Step-by-step explanation of the exercise

❏ Starting from A on the left rein, the rider proceeds in working trot sitting, on a 15m-diameter circle (shown in green), riding a transition to working canter left. They proceed on the long side of the arena in canter, before riding a trot transition at C on a half 15m circle.

❏ The rider approaches the poles in working trot sitting. The first element of the double is jumped from trot, and the second from canter. After jumping the double, the rider rides a transition back to trot before K, and a walk transition at A.

❏ To ride this exercise on the right rein, the jump grid (the poles and the double) need to be reversed, and approached from A. The preceding circle is ridden at C.

❏ This exercise can be viewed from TP1.

❏ This circle is useful for establishing the quality of the canter, namely rhythm, balance and engagement before proceeding straight, on the long side. Check the rider's contact is even, and the outline of the horse is correct.

❏ The purpose of approaching the grid in trot is to ensure the rider is in control and able to approach in a relaxed manner. This gives them time to focus on accuracy, rhythm and balance.

❏ The transitions between trot and canter are important in order to maintain the quality of the horse's gaits, the engagement of the hind-quarters, and to ensure the horse works correctly through its back. If the horse is supple through its body, it will jump with good technique, or bascule, which in turn makes it easy for the rider to maintain a good position in the saddle.

❏ When jumping a double, the non-jumping stride between the fences is important. Look for the rider's upper body position between fences.

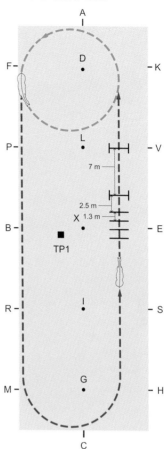

Place four trotting poles set at 1.3m apart on the inside track between S and E. At E, construct a double of two upright fences, with the first at a distance of 2.5m from the last pole and the second element at a distance of 7m from the first fence, for one non-jumping canter stride between them.

TP1 gives a side view of the exercise.

Common faults and how to rectify these

• If the rider leans too far forwards over the fences, the horse may jump awkwardly, unbalancing the rider, which may affect their confidence. Making sure the rider sits up between the two fences enables them to keep this one canter stride balanced, ensuring a successful jump over the second element.

• If the horse refuses the second element, the rider needs to turn the horse away from the fence, and make a new approach. Make sure this is done calmly and with attention to keeping both horse and rider relaxed, so they learn from their experience.

46. CANTER POLES

Aims of the exercise

Establishing a balanced canter over ground poles helps to develop strength through the horse's hind-quarters, improving the 'bounce' of the canter stride, which is required for good jumping technique, or 'bascule', over fences.

Step-by-step explanation of the exercise

❑ Starting from A on the left rein on a half-circle, horse and rider proceed in working trot. Between F and P, they ride a 15m-diameter circle left (shown in green). On this circle a transition to working canter left lead is ridden.

❑ They continue in working canter around the arena, riding a half-circle onto the approach line to the poles after C. After cantering over the poles, a transition to trot is ridden, before returning to the track before A. The exercise can then be repeated.

❑ A change of rein is required to ride this exercise on the right rein, starting from C.

❑ TP1 gives a side view of the poles.

❑ On the circle, which can be repeated as needed, work on the rhythm, balance and engagement of the canter. Proceeding around the arena, make sure the rider maintains sufficient impulsion in the canter for the horse to canter over the poles.

❑ Transitions within the gait are useful in developing the rider's sense of the optimum canter stride for their horse to be able to canter over the poles. Once they have this in mind, and can maintain the 'bounce' in the canter, it will stand them in good stead for future jumping exercises.

Common faults and how to rectify these

• If the canter is not balanced enough when the rider is at S, ask them to turn away from the track before the poles, riding a circle to give the opportunity to improve the canter. Once balanced, they can approach the poles again. Make sure you ask the rider to turn before they commit the horse to the line of poles to avoid any sense of pulling the horse out sharply, which may lead to the horse running out the side on future attempts.

• If the rider's position is not secure, they have insufficient influence over the engagement of the

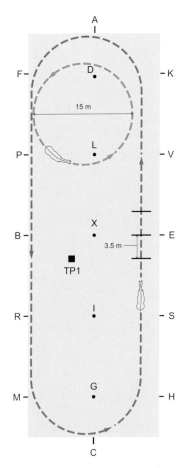

Set three ground poles at a distance of 3.5m apart on the inside track of the long side of the arena, with the middle pole opposite E. This gives the opportunity to approach the poles on both reins.

TP1 gives a side view of the poles.

horse's hind-quarters, resulting in a flatter canter stride. After correcting the rider's position, ask them to focus on the leg sequence of the horse in canter, particularly the moment of suspension over each pole. They should feel the horse's back lift under the saddle, encouraging this further by closing their legs. Also ensure the outline of the horse is correct, and the rider is not restricting the horse's back movement with a strong contact.

TOP TIP

See Exercise 61: Collection/Extension.

47. SINGLE FENCES FROM CANTER

Aims of the exercise

The aim here is to jump single fences on the same rein, with the same canter lead, to consolidate the canter quality.

Step-by-step explanation of the exercise

Placing the fences at A and C 1.5m inside the track allows the rider to ride outside each of these fences as they ride a 15m-diameter circle at each end of the arena.

❑ Starting on the left rein at A in working trot, the rider commences a 15m-diameter circle, on which they establish working canter, left lead. After the circle, they proceed around the arena cantering over fences 1 to 3. They then bring the horse onto a circle at A, riding a transition to working trot on the circle around fence 4.

❑ If this exercise is successful, horse and rider can proceed to jumping all four fences the next time around the arena, again ending with a circle at A, returning to trot.

❑ A change of rein is required to ride this exercise on the right rein, circling around fence 2 and jumping fences 3, 4 and 1.

❑ This exercise combines bending, on the circles, and straightness in preparation for approaching fences. A point to consider is to check the straightness of horse and rider between the fences to ensure the best approach line to each fence.

❑ The circles can be repeated as necessary, using them for transitions within the gait, collecting and lengthening the canter stride, to improve the canter. Also, monitor the quality of the canter, to assess if the rhythm and tempo is optimal for jumping. Walk and trot transitions can also be ridden on the circle to improve balance and responsiveness of the horse to the rider's aids.

❑ When jumping all four fences in succession, the emphasis should be on maintaining the canter rhythm around the whole arena.

Common faults and how to rectify these

• If the rider has difficulty keeping the horse straight between the fences, drifting to one side, check their weight is equal in both stirrups.

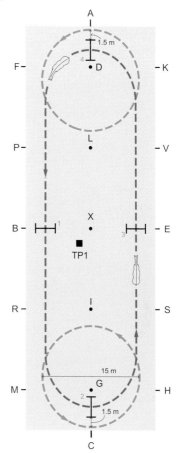

Set four fences, of 0.8m in height, around the arena. The first is on the track, opposite B, the second on the inside track opposite C. The third is on the track, opposite E, and the fourth on the inside track opposite A.

TP1 gives a view if this exercise. If you need to move to get a closer view of horse and rider, move as necessary along the centre line to keep clear of the rider's approach to the fences.

Also make sure their turns through the corners are balanced, that they are not leaning in, and supporting the horse with even rein contact.

• Observe how they straighten the horse with their body position after each turn. Circling around the fences at A and C can be used to clarify how the rider asks the horse to bend.

• If the horse speeds up during this exercise, transitions back to trot for a few strides between the fences can be ridden to maintain control. Regulating the horse's speed on straight lines is necessary when jumping a set course of fences.

48. COURSE RIDING TECHNIQUE

Aims of the exercise

The aim here is to change direction between fences, changing canter lead through trot, and placing the horse accurately on the line of approach to each fence.

Step-by-step explanation of the exercise

❑ Assess the quality of the canter, namely speed and rhythm throughout this short course. Encourage a wide turn from fence 1 to 2, to give the rider plenty of time to plan their approach to fence 2. After fence 2, look for straightness and balance through the change of canter lead through trot (shown in green).

❑ Turning towards fence 3, check the outline of the horse, and the quality of the rein contact. A change of lead through trot is required after fence 3 (shown in green). Assess bend and balance as horse and rider turn from fence 3 to 4. Finally, look for a straight approach to the last fence, with the rider bringing the horse back to trot, and then walk, on a straight line (shown in green), finally halting at K to complete the exercise. This final halt ensures the rider is focusing on all aspects of riding the course, keeping control and balance throughout. After a short rest, they can repeat the exercise.

Common faults and how to rectify these

• There is ample space in this course for the rider to ride large turns at either end of the school. If they have difficulty with the changes of lead through trot, for instance, the horse is going too fast after fence 2 or 3, they have time to steady the canter, and ask again.

• Should the horse become excited in canter, the rider should be encouraged to steady the horse with half-halts. If necessary, a transition from canter, through trot, to walk can be ridden on the large turns at either end of the school, picking up canter again before the next fence.

• If the rider tires, becomes anxious, or has difficulty maintaining canter throughout this exercise, they can jump from trot. Once this is successful, they can try again in canter.

• If the lines of approach need improving, horse and rider can proceed in trot until they are lined up with the centre of the fence, cantering a few strides before the point of take-off.

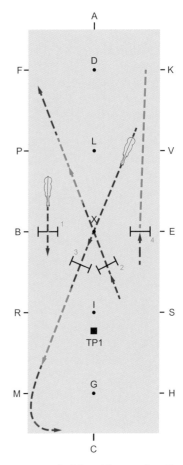

Four fences are needed for this exercise. Fence 1 is on the inside track, opposite B, and fence 2 on the diagonal line HF, jumped towards F on the left rein. Fence 3 is jumped on the diagonal line KM. Fence 4 is on the inside track opposite E. This exercise can be viewed from TP1, to keep clear of the lines of approach.

Horse and rider in balance and harmony over a parallel fence.
Photo courtesy of Maisie Morgan Eventing.

49. SIMPLE COURSE IN CANTER

Aims of the exercise

The aim here is to jump a course in canter, with a change of lead through trot where required, preparing horse and rider for a novice competition.

Step-by-step explanation of the exercise

❏ Starting from A on the left rein in working canter, horse and rider jump fence, keeping straight, before turning off the track towards fence 2, also approached on the left rein, and jumped towards F. A change of leg is required (shown in green) before turning towards fence 3, the double, jumped on the right rein, in right lead canter. Make sure the rider looks for their line of approach to each fence.

❏ Fence 4, on the track at C is jumped from right lead canter, before approaching fence 5, on the diagonal line, MK. A change of lead to left canter is required before K (shown in green). Fence 6, on the track at A, is jumped from left lead canter. This completes the course.

❏ As competition preparation, this exercise should be ridden as though it were a jumping round at an event. Introduce the rider to the idea of the starting point of the course, and riding through the finish, by placing a pair of cones before the first fence, and after the last.

❏ Make sure the rider establishes the correct canter lead, in balance and a suitable tempo for jumping, before approaching each fence. There is space around L for the rider to bring the horse on a circle should they experience a problem with their rhythm and tempo.

❏ After completing the course, the rider can bring the horse back onto a circle around L to ride a transition back to trot, and then to walk on a long rein in order to relax. The course can be repeated as required.

Common faults and how to rectify these

• Riders often become anxious when faced with a course of fences. A way to avoid this is to prepare them well in previous lessons, and not to attempt putting it all together in a course until they feel confident enough.

• If difficulties arise with a particular fence, this can be jumped again on its own, before attempting the whole course again. For example, if jumping the double presented a problem, the rider could

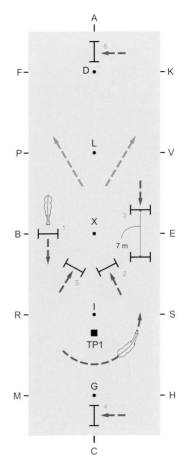

Fence 1 is placed on the inside track at B jumped on the left rein. Fence 2 is also approached on the left rein, jumped towards F, before turning towards fence 3, a double, jumped on the right rein. Fence 4, on the track at C is jumped before approaching fence 5, on the diagonal line, MK. Fence 6, on the track at A, is jumped on the left rein to complete the course. TP1 gives a view of the course while keeping clear of the lines of approach.

circle around the outside of fence 1 and approach the double again, before riding to fence 4, and continuing with the course.

• The rhythm and tempo of the canter is key to a successful round. Problems can arise if the canter quality is poor. If it is too fast, the rider will have difficulty riding with accuracy, and the horse will be unbalanced, and lose confidence in the rider, possibly resulting in run-outs, or refusal of the fences. Make sure the importance of riding between the fences is highlighted to the rider. If the canter rhythm suits both horse, and rider, the course riding will flow, and the jumps will seem easy.

50. COOL-DOWN

Aims of the exercise

The aim here is to cool down, relaxing and stretching the horse in canter after completing a course.

Step-by-step explanation of the exercise

The rider commences a 15m-diameter circle left, in left lead canter, riding inside fence 6, at A. A change of rein is ridden in trot, passing between fence 2 and the second element of the double (shown in green). Right-lead canter is ridden at the C end of the school, passing inside the fence on the track (fence 4), before changing the rein for a second time between fences 1 and 5. A change of leg through trot is required here (shown in green), to right-lead canter, in order to return to the 15m-diameter circle to the left at the A end of the arena.

❑ The rider rides in a light, forwards seat, encouraging the horse to stretch forwards and downwards, easing the reins forwards as the horse lengthens its neck. It is imperative that the rider keeps the horse in balance. Once the horse stretches in canter, a transition to working trot is ridden. Make sure the rider is in rising trot, or in a light seat (standing in the stirrups) to keep their weight off the horse's back. Once the horse is relaxed in trot, ask the rider to bring the horse to walk.

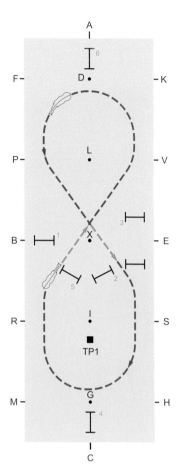

The jump layout is the same as in Exercise 49.

TP1 gives a clear view, staying clear of where horse and rider are riding.

Common faults and how to rectify these

• If the horse has become tense when being ridden around the course, it may not be possible for the rider to ease the reins initially. In this case, they should keep the horse on a contact, and aim at slowing the tempo of the canter with half-halts, before riding a trot transition, also on a contact. If the rider is able to steady the trot sufficiently to ease the contact, they should do so. If not, they can ride a transition to walk, and stretch the horse in walk.

• If the rider is anxious about easing the reins, a useful technique is for them to ease one rein at a time, alternately giving the hand forwards. Once they feel at ease with this, they can allow the horse to stretch.

• Make sure the rider is able to keep their balance in a light seat in canter. If not, they can sit in the saddle, and work on their light seat in trot. They can finish in walk, sitting in the saddle, with the horse on a long rein, the aim being that they are both ending the exercise on a good note.

• It is important to stress to the rider that cooling down, so the horse can relax and stretch, still requires accurate riding, keeping the horse in balance. More trot steps can be taken on the changes of rein, allowing the rider more time to ride with accuracy.

INTERMEDIATE PROPS (20 × 60m ARENA)

51. STRETCHING

Aims of the exercise

The aim of this exercise is to encourage the horse to stretch through the back and neck, while spiralling in and out on circles.

Step-by-step explanation of the exercise

- Starting from A on the left rein in working trot on a long rein, a 20m-diameter circle is ridden around the first cone. Horse and rider then proceed around the arena, riding a 20m-diameter circle commencing at B, around the cone at X. A third circle is ridden around cone 3, and a fourth, commencing at E, around the cone at X. They then proceed on the track to A, from where the exercise can be repeated.
- This exercise can be ridden in walk and canter, with the horse stretching through the back, on both reins. Stretching work can be used anytime during a lesson as required.
- A change of rein is required to ride this exercise on the right rein.
- The rider can spiral in and out around the cones, changing the size of the circles, to increase and decrease lateral bend, in order to develop strength through the back, improve suppleness and encourage relaxation.
- The rein contact should be light, with the reins sufficiently long to invite the horse to stretch forwards and downwards throughout the exercise, facilitating longitudinal stretching through the back.

Common faults and how to rectify these

- It is important for both horse and rider to remain in balance when riding the circles, to make sure they are both able to relax.
- When spiralling in, the correct amount of weight into the inside stirrup encourages the horse to step under the rider's weight, and so spiral in. Too much weight to the inside can cause the horse to fall in.
- Weight into the outside stirrup encourages the horse to adjust its balance to the outside, making it easier for it to spiral out. Too much weight to the outside can cause the horse to drift out.
- Leaning in unbalances the rider's weight distribution in the stirrups, with too much weight on their inside

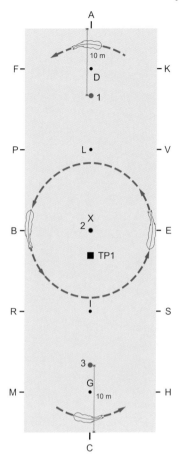

Place three cones on the centre line: the first 10m from the short side at A; the second at X; and the third 10m from C. This exercise can be viewed from TP1.

foot, again affecting the horse's ability to spiral in, causing it to fall in instead, and blocking the inside hind leg from stepping under the body.
- Correct use of the weight aids, however, helps the horse to respond to the rider's outside leg, when spiralling in, and their inside leg aid, when spiralling out.
- If a difference in the horse's suppleness on either rein is detected, the rider's position and balance should be assessed and adjusted, because of the impact this has on the horse's balance.

TOP TIP

Riding in a light seat improves the rider's awareness of weight distribution in the stirrups.

52. USING DRESSAGE LETTERS: IMPROVING ENGAGEMENT

Aims of the exercise

The aim here is to improve engagement of the hind-quarters, developing collection, and to improve accuracy, with each halt/half-halt being executed as the rider's outside knee reaches each letter.

Step-by-step explanation of the exercise

Starting from A on the left rein, horse and rider proceed in working trot sitting around the whole arena, riding into each corner. At each letter a half-halt is ridden. Once this is achieved, a more collected trot can be developed, with a halt transition ridden at the middle letter of each side, A, B, C and E, with half-halts executed at the other letters. A change of rein is required to ride this exercise on the right rein.

❏ Make sure the rider maintains the horse's outline, as each half-halt is executed, using their body and rein aids correctly. As they progress around the school, the quality of the trot should improve, with neither the horse nor rider relying on the contact alone to bring about a rounder frame, with activated haunches, and a rounding of the loins. All these qualities are required for collection, so this exercise is a way to teach the rider how to collect the horse.

❏ Once the trot is sufficiently collected, the rider can proceed to riding a transition to halt at the middle letter of each side of the arena. This exercise progression requires the rider to prepare for each halt with half-halts.

Common faults and how to rectify these

• A common mistake is for the rider to ask the horse to slow down, and speed up again, rather than to engage the horse's haunches. If the rider needs to have a better understanding of the half-halt, ask them to walk a step or two at each letter, before resuming trot. Once this is mastered, ask them to resume a half-halt as their outside knee is level with each letter in turn.

• Also, make sure the corners are ridden correctly, in order to maintain, and improve, the engagement of the haunches. This engagement is helpful in improving the quality of the trot, and developing collection.

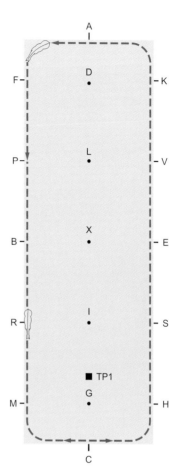

This exercise can be viewed from TP1.

• If difficulties arise when riding a halt transition directly from trot at A, B, C and E, progressive transitions can be ridden, with a couple of walk steps before the halt. Once this is achieved, direct transitions from trot to halt can be resumed.

• After each halt, the direct transition to trot helps to develop impulsion, the 'pushing power' of the haunches. If the horse rushes forwards, make sure the rider is not pushing with their seat, which would push the horse out of balance. If the horse is reluctant to move forwards from the halt, check the rider is not tight in their back, and their leg aids are correct. The rein contact may be too strong in this instance.

53. CONES FOR CIRCLES (15m DIAMETER)

Aims of the exercise

The aim here is to maintain a consistent bend through the horse's body when riding 15m-diameter circles. This helps to develop the accuracy of the rider when riding circles, and the suppleness and balance of the horse.

Step-by-step explanation of the exercise

- ❏ Starting from A on the left rein in walk, ask the rider to proceed on a 15m circle in medium walk around the cones. They should use the cones to define each quarter circle, aiming for the same quality of walk, namely length of stride, rhythm and tempo, as they ride each segment. This exercise is then repeated on the right rein.

- ❏ When riding this exercise in working trot, sufficient engagement should be maintained for the horse to stay in balance around the circle. This helps the rider to understand the concept of collection. Assess the rider's aids and position as they ride the circle to ensure correct technique in maintaining the horse's bend.

- ❏ In canter, this exercise requires the rider to have sufficient knowledge of adjusting the canter stride, both through collection, and lengthening the stride. It tests their ability to maintain the horse's outline with appropriate use of the rein contact by guiding the horse, without restricting the neck, which could impact on the quality of the canter.

Common faults and how to rectify these

- • If the rhythm is inconsistent, ask the rider to count the number of strides taken between each cone as they progress around the circle. They should alter the speed and balance of the walk, trot, or canter as necessary, and have regard for developing collection in each gait to help the horse remain balanced during this exercise.

- • If the horse drifts outwards on the circle, ask the rider to ride at the same distance from each cone, using their outside rein and leg to support the horse.

- • If the horse cuts in too closely to the cones, ask the rider to use their inside leg to support the horse. Also, check if they are leaning in, and if their weight aids into the stirrups are correct.

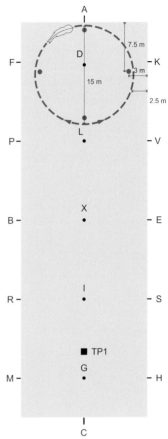

Place four cones, equally spaced, to define a 15m circle, with the first 1.5m in from the track at A. Place a second cone between F and P, 7.5m distance from the short side, and 3m in from the long side. Place a third cone on the centre line 1.5m before L, and a fourth cone between K and V, 7.5m distance from the short side, and 3m in from the long side. This exercise can be viewed from TP1, to assess both the inside and outside of horse and rider.

- • Ensure the rider turns the horse correctly, using each cone as a checkpoint for their position, namely assessing the alignment of their hips and shoulders.

TOP TIP

It can be difficult to centralise a 15m circle from the middle of the short side, at A or C, so a guide is for the sides of the circle to be 2.5m in from the arena edge.

54. CONES FOR DOUBLE LOOPS

Aims of the exercise

The aim here is to use double loops on the long side to test the rider's accuracy and ability to change the horse's flexion and bend through the exercise.

Step-by-step explanation of the exercise

❑ Starting from A on the left rein in medium walk, ask the rider to ride accurately through the corner between A and F, establishing the horse's left flexion and bend. On reaching F, they ride the first loop, inclining from the track, and changing to right flexion and bend, passing the first cone. On returning to the track, left flexion and bend is re-established, before reaching the track at B, completing the first loop.

❑ After B, they ride the second loop, inclining from the track, and changing to right flexion and bend, passing the second cone. On returning to the track, left flexion and bend is re-established, before reaching the track, completing the second loop. They then ride through the corner between M and C, maintaining left flexion and bend. They straighten the horse at C.

❑ The loops can be repeated on the next long side, starting from C, with the mid-point between the loops being at E.

❑ The rider can change direction, to ride the exercise on the right rein. If the exercise is mastered in walk, it can then be ridden in collected trot.

Common faults and how to rectify these

• If the preceding corner to the first loop is not ridden accurately, this will affect the shape of the first loop, so make sure the rider prepares the horse, that is flexion, bend and balance, beforehand, as they pass A on the short side.

• As a guide to correct flexion, ask the rider to make sure the horse's ears are on the line of travel. To keep the rider's upper body correctly aligned, ask them to look between the horse's ears as they progress through the exercise. This avoids any temptation for the rider to turn their head too much, looking around the arena, and lose focus on what the horse is doing.

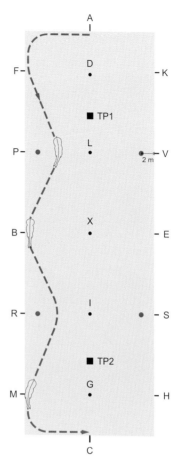

Place two cones on each long side, opposite P, R, S and V, 2m in from the long side. The cones are used to mark the deepest point of each loop. Starting from A on the left rein, a double loop is ridden on the long side, using the cones for accuracy, to ensure both loops are ridden the same shape and depth. The mid-point between the loops is on the track at B.

View the exercise, moving between TP1 and TP2 as necessary.

• When riding this exercise in collected trot, ensure the rider uses half-halts to prepare the horse for each change of flexion and bend in order to maintain and improve the quality of the collected trot.

TOP TIP

This exercise can also be ridden in collected canter to develop counter-canter.

55. CONES FOR LEG YIELD

Aims of the exercise

This exercise aims to introduce horse and rider to the concept of leg-yield, travelling sideways on a diagonal line.

Step-by-step explanation of the exercise

❑ Starting from K on the left rein, in medium walk, the rider positions the horse to the left, as they reach the first cone, turning onto the line of travel from A to B (shown in green). Maintaining left position, leg yield left is ridden to the cone opposite B, where the horse is straightened, proceeding straight around the arena, returning to A, from where the exercise can be repeated.

❑ After changing the rein, the exercise can be repeated with leg yield right being ridden, commencing from the cone at A and finishing by the cone at E.

❑ Once achieved in walk, the exercise can be ridden in collected trot. When ridden in canter, this is a very effective exercise in developing engagement, that is the loading of the inside hind leg as it steps forwards and across, under the horse's midline, or centre of gravity.

❑ Check the consistency of flexion and bend as the exercise is ridden, paying attention to the beginning, and end, of the leg yield, as to how the rider prepares the horse for these transitions between going straight and travelling sideways.

Common faults and how to rectify these

• With leg yield, the aim is for the horse to step forwards and sideways along its line of travel, while maintaining balance, moving away from the rider's inside leg. The rider maintains flexion and bend by supporting the horse with their body position and rein contact.

• Check that the rider has correct left position in their body, with their inside leg by the girth, with pressure to ask the horse to move away from the leg, and the outside leg behind the girth, maintaining the alignment of the haunches. A common mistake is to move the inside leg too far back when asking for leg yield, effectively displacing the horse's haunches. This results in the horse drifting sideways rather than remaining in balance.

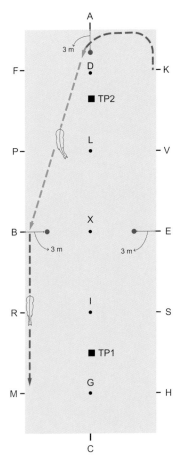

Place one cone 3m in from the track at A, a second 3m in from the track at B, and a third 3m in from the track at E.

TP1 gives a view of the leg yield from A. TP2 views leg yield from C.

• If the horse has too much neck bend, check if the rider has too much inside rein contact, or has lost contact on their outside rein. Both these result in the horse falling out through its outside shoulder, losing engagement of the inside hind leg.

• If the rider leans to the inside (of the bend of the horse), the horse will drift too much sideways, resulting from a loss of balance.

TOP TIP

The degree of bend is relative to the suppleness of the horse. Leg yield can be ridden with the horse straight, or with more bend in the ribs as for shoulder-in.

56. CONES FOR TURN ON/AROUND THE FOREHAND

Aims of the exercise

The aim here is using a cone to ride around helping the rider to keep the horse on the spot as it turns, and to distinguish between turn *on* the forehand, as opposed to a turn *around* the forehand.

Step-by-step explanation of the exercise

Place one cone 5m in from the track at V, and a second 5m in from the track at S.

❏ Starting from A on the left rein in collected walk, horse and rider proceed on the track, turning left just before P. On reaching the first cone, a turn on the forehand is ridden, by moving the horse's body to the left, maintaining right bend.

❏ They then proceed straight across the centre line, turning left on reaching the track before B. Just before R, they turn left. On reaching the second cone, they repeat the turn on the forehand before proceeding straight across the arena to the long side, turning left on reaching the track. The exercise can be repeated on the right rein by commencing from C.

❏ To ride a turn *on* the forehand around each cone, make sure the rider brings the horse to a halt as they reach the cone. In the halt, they should then correctly position the horse before commencing each turn on the forehand. After the turn, they bring the horse to a halt, straighten it, and proceed straight across the school. This turn is more static than a turn *around* the forehand.

❏ To ride a turn *around* the forehand around each cone, the rider collects the walk before reaching the cone. In collected walk, they turn around the cone, before proceeding straight across the school. This turn is larger than a turn on the forehand. Look for the rhythm of the collected walk being maintained, and the use of half-halts to set the horse up for the turn.

❏ With both styles of turn, the rider asks for the horse to step sideways by the girth with their inside leg. Their outside leg is used behind the girth, to guard the haunches, preventing them from swinging out. Both horse and rider should remain consistently in left position throughout both turn options.

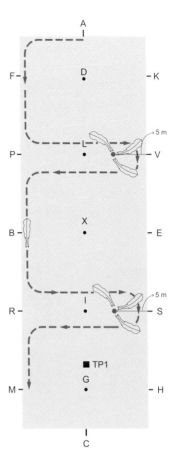

Place one cone 5m in from the track at V, and a second 5m in from the track at S.

TP1 gives a good view of the whole arena.

Common faults and how to rectify these

• One difficulty the rider may experience when riding the turn *on* the forehand, is that the horse 'sticks' in the halt. If this happens, they can ride the larger option of a turn *around* the forehand where no halt is required. This is a way to maintain the forward impetus of the horse when turning.

• If the horse lacks collection and balance, drifting away from the rider's inside leg when riding a turn *around* the forehand, then a turn *on* the forehand may help to establish control for the rider, with the use of a halt before and after the turn.

57. POLES FOR SHOULDER-IN

Aims of the exercise

The aim here is for the placement of poles to help the rider to learn the requirements of riding shoulder-in.

Step-by-step explanation of the exercise

For this exercise, three poles are required, set 3m in from the long side of the arena, opposite P, B and R.

❑ Starting from A on the left rein, in collected walk, the rider rides shoulder-in left on the long side, between P and R (shown in green), using the poles to help align the angle of the horse to the wall, aiding consistency of the movement. They then proceed straight around the arena to the next long side, riding shoulder-in between S and V (also shown in green) without the supporting poles.

❑ Assess the quality of the collected walk, the riding of the arena corners, and the correctness of the positioning of the horse on approaching P. It can be suggested to the rider that they use the poles as a guide to keeping the horse on the line of travel, with the horse flexed towards the poles on a consistent angle. After R, on completing the shoulder-in, note how the rider resumes straightness in the track before they proceed around the arena.

❑ When riding shoulder-in on the next long side, between S and V, assess how the rider keeps the horse on the track with their position, and the application of their inside leg, asking the horse to step forwards and sideways, and the support of their outside rein and leg, maintaining the angle of the shoulder-in. Check their preparation for the shoulder-in, using half-halts, and how they straighten the horse at V.

❑ Once achieved in collected walk, this exercise can be ridden in collected trot, and also in collected canter, developing collection, namely the lowering of the haunches, and the elevation of the forehand.

❑ A change of rein is required to ride this exercise on the right rein.

Common faults and how to rectify these

• Lateral work, such as shoulder-in, is a progression from developing correct flexion, bend and straightness. For this reason, reminding the rider to pay attention to how they ride around the

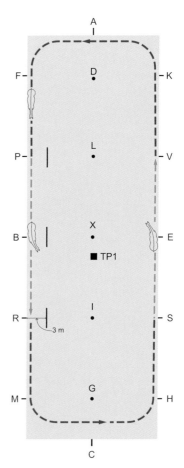

For this exercise, three poles are required, set 3m in from the long side of the arena, opposite P, B and R.

The exercise can be viewed from TP1, rotating as required.

arena, namely corners, and how straight they ride on the track, prepares the horse for riding the sections of shoulder-in in this exercise.

• When riding this exercise in collected trot, or canter, make sure the rhythm and length of stride is consistent before, during and after the shoulder-in. This tests the rider's feel for the horse's natural rhythm – as pushing the horse out of this, by riding too fast, is likely to cause tension, affecting the quality of the contact and balance.

TOP TIP

Riding a change of rein in extended walk, or medium trot, helps to maintain the forwardness of the horse, refreshing the energy of collected walk, and the impulsion of collected trot and canter.

58. POLES FOR CHANGES OF REIN (DIRECTION) ACROSS THE ARENA

Aims of the exercise

The aim here is to use poles to mark out changes of rein across the arena, defining the combination of straight lines across the centre line, and the turns away from, and onto, the track, to challenge the accuracy of horse and rider.

Step-by-step explanation of the exercise

❏ Starting from A on the left rein, in medium, or collected, walk, the rider proceeds on the track to P. At P, they turn left, passing between the two parallel poles at L. On reaching the track at V, they turn right. On turning right again at S, they proceed to pass between the parallel poles on the centre line at I. On reaching the track at R, they turn left onto the track, proceeding around the corner to C, to complete the exercise.

❏ A change of rein is needed to ride the mirror-image of this exercise, starting on the right rein at A.

❏ This exercise can be made more challenging by adding a transition to halt between both sets of parallel poles, which are used to check the straightness of both horse and rider.

❏ Once mastered in medium or collected walk, it can be ridden in collected trot, with a few walk steps between the parallel poles, and a transition to halt on the track at B and E.

❏ When ridden in collected canter, a simple change through collected walk can be ridden between each pair of parallel poles and a half-halt, to check balance, by the poles at B and E.

Common faults and how to rectify these

• Cutting the corners, with the horse falling in, affects the accurate placement of the straight lines across the centre line, which is where the parallel poles are helpful, by giving the rider a focal point to ride to.

• When riding between the pole at B and the wall, the rider can use half-halts to develop the horse's

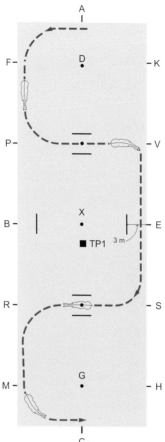

A pair of parallel poles is laid on the centre line, either side of L. A second pair is laid either side of I. Both pairs are set at 3m apart. On the long sides, a pole is set 3m in from the track opposite B, and another 3m in from the track opposite E.

This exercise can be viewed from TP1, rotating as necessary.

collection, namely engagement of the haunches. This is also a useful place to check that the horse is ridden straight for a few steps in between the changes of flexion and bend required when riding the turns (corners). This is replicated when riding between the pole at E and the wall.

• If the horse loses the forward impulse when ridden in collection, make sure the rider rides the horse in extended walk, medium trot, or medium canter in order to generate swing through the back.

59. POLES FOR THREE-LOOP SERPENTINES

Aims of the exercise

This exercise aims at perfecting a serpentine, being a series of connected curved lines. Poles are used to ensure the loops are ridden in the same shape and depth to the long sides.

Step-by-step explanation of the exercise

❑ Starting from A on the left rein in medium walk, horse and rider pass by the pole between F and P, which marks the deepest point of the first serpentine loop. They proceed to the parallel poles between X and I, riding a horse's length straight (3–4 strides), before continuing onto the second loop, with its deepest point at E, marked here by the pole. On completing the second loop, they ride between the parallel poles between L and X, riding a horse's length straight (3–4 strides). They then proceed onto the third serpentine loop, with its deepest point by the pole between R and M. The serpentine is completed at C.

❑ Once mastered in medium walk, this exercise can be ridden in working trot, walking for a horse's length between each pair of parallel poles. It can be ridden in collected canter, with a change of canter lead through trot, or walk, between these poles.

❑ After a change of rein, this exercise can be ridden on the right rein, starting at A.

Common faults and how to rectify these

• The poles placed near the track, marking the deepest point of each loop, help the rider to ride each loop an even shape, with the curve before, and after, these poles being identical. They help to prevent the shape of the loops being flattened, with the horse falling in. The poles across the centre line give the rider a focal point to aim for when riding across the centre line.

• To ride the serpentine fluently, the horse's rhythm and balance need to be consistent throughout this exercise. The speed of each gait used also affects fluency, so the rider needs to judge the most suitable tempo for the horse.

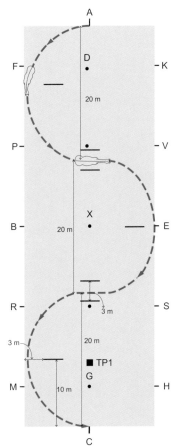

Place a single pole, with one end 3m in from the track, at a distance of 10m from the short side of the A end of the arena (between F and P). Place a second pole, with one end opposite E, 3m in from the track. A third pole is laid correspondingly, between R and M, 10m from the short side at the C end of the arena. In addition, a pair of parallel poles, 3m apart, is placed across the centre line at a distance of 20m from A. A second pair of parallel poles is laid similarly across the centre line, 20m from C.

The exercise can be viewed from TP1, staying clear of the horse's line of travel.

TOP TIP

This exercise can also be ridden in canter to further the quality of counter-canter.

60. COMBINATION PROPS FOR ACCURACY

Aims of the exercise

The aim here is to consolidate movements learned through the previous exercises at intermediate level.

Step-by-step explanation of the exercise

❏ Starting from A in collected walk, the rider rides leg yield, inclining across the school from A to P. On reaching P, they ride shoulder-in to R. The positioning of the horse should be the same for both movements (shown in green). At R, they commence a 15m-diameter circle. On returning to R, they proceed around the school to H, where they ride a double loop, with the first from H to E, passing around the cone, and the second from E to K, also passing around the cone.

❏ Once mastered in walk – using both medium for the 15m-diameter circle, and collected walk, for the lateral work and shallow loops – it can be ridden in trot. The lateral work can be ridden in collected trot, with working trot for the circle and loops. In canter, the lateral work, and shallow loops, can be ridden in collected canter, with the 15m-diameter circle ridden in working canter.

❏ The exercise can then be repeated from A. A change of rein is required to ride the exercise on the right rein, starting from A.

Common faults and how to rectify these

• If the rider loses confidence when attempting the whole exercise in one go, spend time working on the individual elements, before putting them together again.

• When riding the transition from leg yield, inclining to the track, to shoulder-in on the track at P, ensure the rider maintains the bend and flexion of the horse. Also, the rider needs to be mindful of the rhythm of the gait, and overall balance of the horse for a seamless transition. This applies to all three gaits.

• The 15m-diameter circle is useful for making sure both horse and rider are relaxed, using working gaits, offering a reprise between the lateral work and the shallow loops. In this way, the whole exercise challenges horse and rider, without causing tension by asking too much for too long.

• When riding the shallow loops in canter, make sure the rider rides the line of travel accurately,

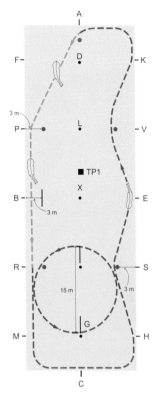

Place one cone 3m in from the track at A, and another 3m in from R. On the next long side, place one cone 3m in from the track opposite S, and another opposite V. Place two poles on the centre line to mark out a 15m-diameter circle, passing outside the poles.

The exercise can be viewed from TP1.

and does not allow the horse to drift in from, and back to, the track. This is a good exercise to improve counter-canter, where the rider needs to be mindful of their position in the saddle dictating the canter lead required.

It is important to check the horse's straightness at intervals to consolidate progress from riding a combination of exercises.

ADVANCED DRESSAGE (20 × 60m ARENA)

61. CIRCLES (10m DIAMETER)

Aims of the exercise

The aim here is to perfect riding 10m-diameter circles.

Step-by-step explanation of the exercise

Starting from A on the left rein, horse and rider proceed in medium walk. Just before, P, the walk is collected, before riding a 10m-diameter circle (shown in green). On returning to the track, a transition to medium walk is ridden. On approaching R, the walk is collected, prior to riding a second 10m-diameter circle at R (shown in green). On completing this circle, a transition to medium walk is ridden, with horse and rider proceeding straight around the arena. The circles can be repeated on the next long side at S and V.

❑ If this is successful, the exercise can be ridden in working and collected trot, and working and collected canter. A change of rein is required to ride the circles on the right rein.

❑ The rider's preparation for each circle should be assessed. When working on the left rein, they should be expected to flex the horse to the left, positioning it for the circle. The smaller the circle, the more bend is required through the horse's body, so ensure the rider's body position corresponds to the bend of the horse in order to maintain balance. When working on the right rein, right flexion and bend should be maintained.

❑ There should be no loss of rhythm as the rider commences the 10m-diameter circles. Whether they are working in walk, trot, or canter, the tempo of the gait should be such that this can be maintained when horse and rider both commence each circle, and return to the track afterwards.

❑ The horse should be ridden straight on the track between the circles, in order to ease the muscles, and to ensure it is working correctly through the back. The quality of the gait can be monitored, before preparing for the second circle.

Common faults and how to rectify these

• A misconception for the rider is to increase the horse's neck bend when riding smaller circles.

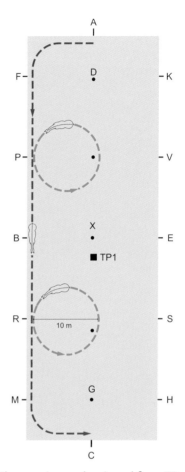

The exercise can be viewed from TP1.

Ensure an even rein contact is maintained, and avoid too strong a contact on the inside rein. On a correctly ridden circle, the rider should be able to release the inside rein contact without the horse losing balance.

• If the horse is not supported with the rider's outside rein and leg, there is a risk of the horse drifting out, affecting the accuracy, size and shape of the circles.

• Inaccurately ridden circles affect the smoothness of the transitions on and off the track, by affecting the horse's balance, engagement of the haunches and its confidence in the rider. The rider should be advised to correct these issues by returning to the walk when riding the circles. A useful adaptation for this exercise is to proceed in collected trot on the track, riding each circle in collected walk.

When riding smaller circles, the flexion and bend of the horse is increased.

62. COLLECTION/EXTENSION

Aims of the exercise

The aim here is to develop collection and extension in all three gaits.

Step-by-step explanation of the exercise

Starting on the left rein from A in collected walk, horse and rider proceed around the arena to P. At P they turn onto the diagonal line towards S (shown in green), in extended walk to S (shown in green).

- ❏ On approaching the track at S, they ride a transition to collected walk, then proceeding straight around the arena to R in collected walk. At R, they turn onto the diagonal line towards V, in extended walk (shown in green).

- ❏ On approaching the track at V, a transition to collected walk is ridden, then proceed around the arena in collected walk.

- ❏ Once achieved in walk, this exercise can be ridden in trot, with collected trot ridden on the track, and extended trot on the diagonal lines. The timing of the upward transition is important. Ensure the rider has completed the turn onto the diagonal lines before asking the horse to extend. This ensures the horse is absolutely straight as impulsion increases. The downward transition from extended to collected trot should be achieved before reaching the track, so the horse is sufficiently balanced for the turn.

- ❏ When riding this exercise in canter, the rider should allow sufficient time to bring the horse back to collected canter before reaching the track at the end of each diagonal line in order to maintain the balance and engagement of the haunches.

Common faults and how to rectify these

- • If the rider pushes the horse out of its natural rhythm in walk by increasing speed, the horse may break into trot. If this happens, ask the rider to re-establish a slower tempo in collected walk so that the horse relaxes, ensuring the outline is correct, and the horse has not become tense to the contact.

- • Similarly, if it is pushed out of rhythm in trot, there is a risk the horse will break into canter. If the canter is not balanced, and engagement maintained when extending the stride, the horse

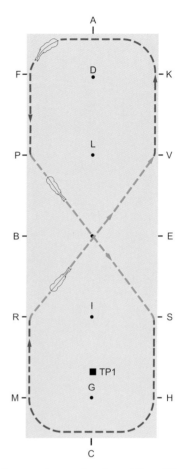

The exercise can be viewed from TP1.

may fall onto its forehand, and break into trot. So often, riders confuse impulsion with speed, so asking the rider to think about slowing the tempo as they ask for extension can help.

- • If the extended canter is too fast, the rider will have difficulty riding the transition from extended to collected canter. As with extending the trot stride, asking the rider to think of slowing the tempo as they ask for extended canter can help.

- • To avoid the horse becoming tense in extended gaits, the rider should be encouraged to maintain a supportive contact, while allowing the horse to extend its frame. Restriction of the neck in walk, trot and canter, will affect the horse's ability to work with impulsion, through its back, creating tension.

63. REIN-BACK

Aims of the exercise

To establish correct technique when riding rein-back.

Step-by-step explanation of the exercise

Starting from A on the left rein in medium walk, horse and rider change the rein from F to E. On this diagonal line, the walk is collected on approach to L. At L, a halt transition is ridden, prior to riding rein-back for one horse's length (3–4 steps, shown in green). After the rein-back, they proceed in medium walk to E, and turn onto the diagonal line from E to M. On approach to I, the walk is collected, with a halt transition ridden at I. A second rein-back is ridden, for one horse's length (shown in green), before proceeding in medium walk to M.

❑ The exercise can be repeated from H to B, and from B to K, with rein-back ridden at I and L.

❑ Once achieved in walk, it can be ridden in trot and canter.

❑ As preparation for the rein-back, the rider should ask the horse to halt in balance. Ensure a still halt is established, with the horse relaxed, and paying full attention to the rider's aids. This enables the rider to ask for rein-back with subtle aids. Once 3–4 steps of rein-back are complete, the rider could ask the horse to halt again, before proceeding forwards, to ensure balance and attention, pre-empting any anticipation by the horse.

❑ In order to prepare for each rein-back, ensure the rider's technique for collecting the horse is correct, particularly the timing and application of half-halts.

❑ The rein contact should be eased as the horse steps backwards. This ensures the horse maintains a correctly rounded frame, with its neck reaching forwards to the bit as it tucks its loins, with the hind legs under its body.

Common faults and how to rectify these

• Crookedness in rein-back can occur if the horse is not absolutely straight. The rider must be reminded of the importance of a square halt, with both hind legs taking equal weight, before asking the horse to step backwards.

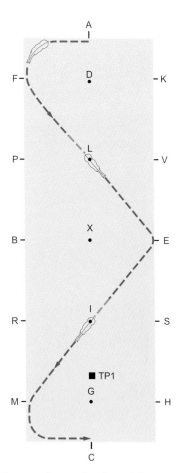

The exercise can be viewed from TP1.

• Using too strong a rein contact when asking for rein-back may displace the horse's haunches to one side. Make sure the concept of rein-back is asking the horse to step forwards into a restraining hand, not pulling back with the hands.

• Sitting too heavily in the saddle can cause the horse to hollow its back when stepping backwards. However, lightening the seat, with the rider inclining the upper body slightly forwards, enables the horse to maintain a rounded outline in rein-back.

TOP TIP

A more demanding variation is to repeat rein-back a second time before proceeding forwards. This is a test of the correctness of the rider's aids, and the horse's suppleness through the back.

64. SERPENTINE (FOUR LOOPS)

Aims of the exercise

To establish accuracy when riding a four-loop serpentine.

Step-by-step explanation of the exercise

Starting from A on the left rein, in medium walk, a four-loop serpentine is ridden. Each loop should be 15m in diameter, and horse and rider should cross the centre line straight for a few steps for 5m, in between each loop.

- On riding the four-loop serpentine in walk, the medium walk should be regular, in that the rider is mindful of maintaining rhythm and length of stride throughout.
- In trot, riding the loops in collected trot can improve accuracy. The strides across the centre line can be ridden more forwards in working trot to improve impulsion. Alternately, this could be ridden in collected walk to work on engagement.
- This exercise can also be ridden in collected canter with a change of canter lead through walk over the centre line. This demands balance and accuracy to maintain fluency. Straightness is important for the change of lead, whether ridden through trot or walk, in order to maintain the engagement of the horse's hind-quarters.
- Regardless of which gait the serpentine is ridden in, straightness over the centre line is required. The technique of riding a serpentine is that the rider changes the horse from the old bend to new bend with a few straight steps in between, so allowing 5m gives time for this.

Common faults and how to rectify these

- If the horse is lacking suppleness, there is a risk of loss of balance on the loops. To work on suppleness through this exercise, ask the rider to add a 15m-diameter circle within each, or some of, the loops as necessary.
- Going too fast affects both the quality of the chosen gait and makes accuracy difficult. Should the horse become tense, being pushed out of its natural rhythm, this tension will impact on its ability to bend around the loops, resulting in crookedness.

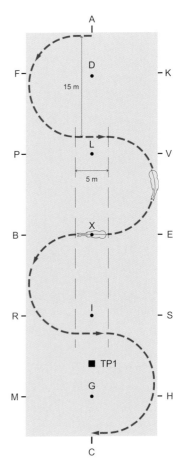

The exercise can be viewed from TP1.

The rider should be informed of the relativity of speed to suppleness and relaxation throughout this exercise.

- Another risk of going too fast is a lack of straightness across the centre line with the horse overshooting each loop, resulting in uneven loops, with the serpentine lacking consistency of shape. Riding forwards calmly is the key.

> ## TOP TIP
>
> If horse and rider are confident and proficient enough in collected canter, a flying change can be ridden across the centre line each time, to change the canter lead. (*See* Exercise 67: Flying Changes)

65. TRAVERS/RENVERS

Aims of the exercise

The aim here is to improve collection by riding travers and renvers.

Step-by-step explanation of the exercise

Starting from A on the left rein in collected walk, a 10m-diameter circle is ridden at F. Between F and R, the rider brings the horse into travers (shown in green). From R to H they proceed straight around the track. At H, a second 10m-diameter circle is ridden, with the rider bringing the horse into renvers (shown in blue) from H to V. After V, they proceed straight around the track, repeating the exercise on reaching A.

❑ A change of rein is required to ride the exercise on the right rein. Once achieved in walk, this exercise can be ridden in collected trot. When riding this exercise in canter, travers can be ridden instead of renvers between H and V, the reason being to avoid a change of canter lead.

❑ With both travers (haunches in) and renvers (haunches out), make sure the horse is ridden on three tracks in order to maintain consistency of bend. This helps the horse to sustain the lowering of its haunches, thus developing collection.

❑ Ensure the rider is able to co-ordinate their seat, leg and rein aids accordingly, with their outside leg asking the horse to step sideways and their inside leg supporting. The inside rein asks, and maintains, flexion, with the outside rein supporting.

❑ Regarding their weight aids, the rider should sit on both seat bones in order to engage both hind legs, with slightly more weight into their inside stirrup, in the direction of travel.

Common faults and how to rectify these

• If too much neck bend is asked for, the horse is likely to fall onto its inside shoulder, affecting regularity of its steps. This can have a knock-on effect for the haunches, with the horse unable to step evenly across behind, thus losing engagement. The horse will travel sideways quite easily, but the quality of collection will be lost.

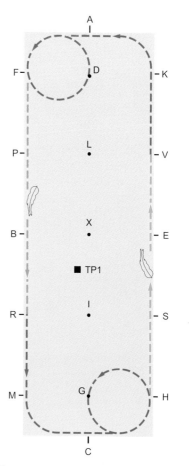

The exercise can be viewed from TP1.

• Using too much outside rein blocks the flexibility of the horse and the freedom of its shoulders, which is necessary for the crossing of the forelegs. In turn, this affects the crossing of the hind legs. The outside rein should support, but not be so strong to prevent the horse from bending.

• Asking for too much angle, in both renvers and travers, can displace the hands to the inside.

• If the horse is seen to be tipping its head to one side, this suggests uneven rein contact. To rectify this, ensure the rider can give either hand forwards, releasing the contact, to check if they have the horse correctly balanced with their seat and legs, and are not over-reliant on the reins to position the horse.

66. HALF-PASS

Aims of the exercise

The aim here is to develop the quality of half-pass, building on the flexibility and strength of the horse.

Step-by-step explanation of the exercise

Starting from A on the left rein in collected walk, a 10m-diameter circle is ridden at F. The rider brings the horse into half-pass from F to X (shown in green). On reaching X, they proceed straight on the centre line, tracking left at C. The exercise can be repeated with a 10m-diameter circle at H, and half-pass ridden from H to X, proceeding straight on the centre line to A.

❑ A change of rein is required to repeat the exercise on the right rein. This exercise can be ridden in walk, trot and canter.

❑ When this exercise is ridden in walk and trot, look for even crossing of both front and hind legs. This indicates the rider has the horse correctly balanced with appropriate use of their seat, rein and leg aids. The bend of the horse should be consistent on both reins, with half-pass right and left being a mirror image of each other.

❑ Look for the rider positioning the horse's ears on the line of travel. The bend of the horse in the half-pass should be the same as that established on the circle. In regard to the rider's aids, their outside leg asks for sideways movement, while the inside leg supports. On reaching the centre line, ensure the rider straightens the horse, maintaining a slight positioning to the left in preparation for turning left at C.

❑ Half-pass is often easier for horse and rider to achieve, and the horse jumps sideways with each canter stride, rather than crossing its legs, as with walk and trot.

Common faults and how to rectify these

• If the outside leg aids are too strong, the haunches may be displaced to the inside (of the bend of the horse), thus the horse avoids taking weight behind, and falls onto its inside shoulder. This can

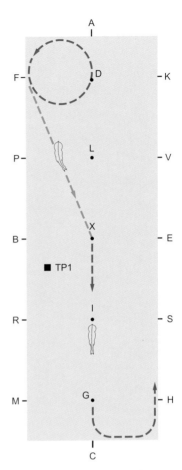

The exercise can be viewed from TP1.

affect regularity, that is the inside foreleg takes a shorter stride than the outside fore.

• Using too strong an inside rein aid can have a similar result. To correct this, make sure the rider uses subtle weight aids, stepping down into their inside stirrup to encourage sideways movement, rather than excessive inside rein/outside leg aids.

• Leaning to the inside causes the horse to fall onto its inside shoulder, disengaging the hind legs. Too much weight on the outside seat bone can overload the outside hind leg, resulting in blocking it from crossing. To correct this, make sure the rider sits centrally, and upright in the saddle without leaning to one side. Their shoulder should be level, as should the horse's ears.

67. COUNTER-CANTER/FLYING CHANGES

Aims of the exercise

This exercise is aimed at using counter canter to develop the quality of the flying change.

Step-by-step explanation of the exercise

Starting from A on the left rein in collected canter left, horse and rider turn onto the diagonal line FE. At E, they proceed on the track in counter-canter (shown in green) to S, riding a half 20m-diameter circle, still in counter-canter, S to R. On reaching R, they turn onto the diagonal line, R to V, executing a flying change from left lead to right lead over the centre line (shown in blue). They proceed in counter-canter (right lead) reaching the track at V, and continuing on the track to K, where a flying change from right lead to left, shown in blue, can be ridden to conclude the exercise.

- ❏ The most important aspect of this exercise is the quality of the collected canter. If the canter has sufficient impulsion, engagement and balance, the rider will be able to maintain left canter throughout the movements shown. It can be helpful to the rider to clarify that the technique of counter-canter is simply to maintain the same canter lead around the arena, and across the diagonal, without allowing the horse to change lead. If they maintain their position, and the horse's balance, this is possible.

- ❏ To execute the flying change, horse and rider need to be completely straight, with an even rein contact. It takes three strides to make a flying change: the step before, with the horse and rider in left position; the straight stride preparing for the change; and the third stride where the rider changes their position to the right, producing the change of lead. The timing of this is crucial for a clean change, during the moment of suspension.

Common faults and how to rectify these

- • When riding counter-canter, the horse can become disunited, changing leg behind, or falling into trot, if the rider has not established a balanced, collected canter. To rectify this, some transitions – walk-canter-walk – can help to improve the horse's balance.

- • If the canter is ridden too forwards, this can render the horse unbalanced, another reason for the canter, again, becoming disunited.

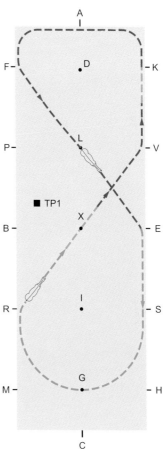

The exercise can be viewed from TP1.

- • If a flying change is late behind, the rider's timing of the aids could be at fault, so working on the rhythm and tempo of the canter can help the rider to identify the moment of suspension. Their aids for the change should be applied as this moment commences, rather like taking off over a jump.

- • Sometimes the horse may anticipate the rider's aids. To avoid this, intersperse this exercise with stretching, to help both horse and rider relax prior to attempting again.

TOP TIP

Counter-canter is key to being able to ride good flying changes. *Preventing* the horse from changing lead ensures a good quality flying change to follow, when the rider *allows* the change to happen.

68. HALF-PIROUETTES

Aims of the exercise

The aim here is to develop the technique of riding half-pirouettes in walk and canter as a foundation for progressing to full pirouettes.

Step-by-step explanation of the exercise

Starting from A on the left rein in collected walk, horse and rider turn left across the arena between F and P. On reaching the quarter line, the rider brings the horse into a half-pirouette. Returning across the centre line, they turn left on the track, before P. On reaching R, they turn left again, across the arena. On reaching the quarter line, the rider brings the horse into a second half-pirouette.

❑ A change of rein is required to repeat the exercise on the right rein. This exercise can be ridden in walk and canter.

❑ When riding half-pirouettes in walk, make sure the rider has the horse correctly positioned before commencing. The rhythm and tempo of the walk should be maintained throughout the pirouette, which consists of between three and four strides, with the hind legs describing a small half-circle, and the forehand moving around the haunches. The walk quality should be consistent both before and after the pirouette.

❑ Whether riding half-pirouettes in walk or canter, check the rider's position is correct, remaining in balance when turning with slight weight into the inside stirrup to help the horse to turn on the spot, with the circle as small as possible. Make sure the horse is correctly collected, with a supportive contact maintaining outline and flexion.

❑ The canter half-pirouette should also consist of three to four strides. Check the consistency of the height, or bounce, of each stride, and the rider's ability to turn in balance with the horse.

Common faults and how to rectify these

• One difficulty is that the horse becomes 'stuck behind' with the hind legs failing to maintain the canter strides. This can happen if the rider asks for too small a turn for the quality of collection, resulting in the horse spinning on the spot with the hind legs stepping together. This fault can be rectified by riding a larger half-pirouette, with the

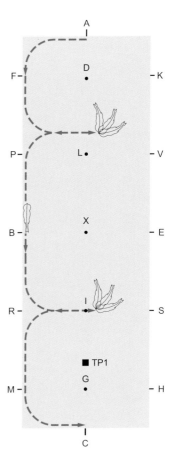

The exercise can be viewed from TP1.

priority being to maintain the horse's rhythm and balance. However, the rider must make sure they do not lose the haunches to the outside, which could result in a half-circle being ridden, and not a half-pirouette.

• If the collected canter lacks impulsion, the horse may fall out of canter. Make sure the rider maintains rhythm and balance prior to, and after, the pirouette.

• On completion of a half-pirouette, a common mistake is for the rider to not pay attention to the first stride afterwards. Failing to ride this stride accurately can result in the horse becoming crooked, or drifting off the line of travel.

TOP TIP

Working on both travers, and shoulder-in, on circles of varying sizes helps the rider to develop feel for the balance and quality of riding half-pirouettes, both in walk and canter.

69. PASSAGE

Aims of the exercise

The aim here is to establish the foundations of passage, developing the horse's strength and athleticism, and the rider's skills in understanding this movement.

Step-by-step explanation of the exercise

Starting from A on the left rein in collected trot, horse and rider proceed on the track to R. At R, they turn left, riding a few steps of passage (shown in green) across the centre line. On reaching S, they turn left again, riding collected trot on the track to V. On reaching V, they turn left again, with a few steps of passage (shown in green) ridden across the centre line. On reaching the track at P, they turn left again, forming a square. To conclude the exercise, medium trot is ridden on a half 20m-diameter circle from R to S (shown in blue).

❑ A change of rein is required to ride the exercise on the right rein.

❑ Make sure the collected trot is of good quality, namely regarding rhythm, tempo and engagement. The rider's rein contact must be supportive, and should be released when true balance is achieved.

❑ As the rider uses half-halts to bring the horse into passage over the centre line, the horse should lower its haunches, rounding its loins, and thus raising the forehand. Check the rider is bracing their back correctly, and closing the thighs to contain the forward impulse of the horse. Medium trot is used to refresh impulsion, and the horse's desire to go forwards.

Common faults and how to rectify these

• A common mistake is the rider expects the horse to go forwards to the detriment of the elevation in passage. The result is a rather stilted movement as a result of losing the suppleness of the horse's back. To rectify this, interspersing passage with medium trot helps to maintain the cadence of the trot as the horse becomes more collected. Treating passage as a collected version of medium trot can be a helpful concept for the rider.

• In order to give the impression of raising the forehand, the rider may mistakenly raise their hands to lift the horse's head so its poll is the highest point. If this happens, the horse will be tight and hollow in the back, producing stilted steps in passage. This issue can be addressed by stretching the horse through its back

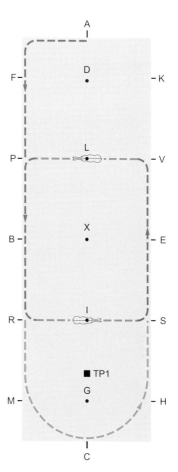

The exercise can be viewed from TP1.

(see Exercise 31, Stretching) to make sure it works correctly though its back, and that the rider understands this concept.

• A laboured passage can indicate that the horse is tired. Signs of tiredness are the horse's feet dragging on the ground, and the rider needing to work hard to produce passage. Make sure this exercise is interspersed with more simple movements, to ensure neither horse nor rider is fatigued.

Developing passage requires a combination of collection and impulsion, which prepares the horse for extended trot.

70. PIAFFE

Aims of the exercise

The aim here is to establish the foundations of piaffe, beginning with half steps, to develop the horse's strength and ability to lower the haunches, and the rider's skills in understanding this movement.

Step-by-step explanation of the exercise

Starting from A on the left rein in collected walk, horse and rider turn left at P. Over the centre line, they ride a few steps of piaffe (shown in green), before proceeding straight, to the track at V. At V, they track right, and at S turn right. Over the centre line, they ride a few steps of piaffe (shown in green), before proceeding straight, to the track at R. At R, they track left, proceeding straight around the arena to C. This exercise can be repeated, starting from C.

- ❏ A change of rein is required to repeat the exercise on the right rein.

- ❏ Primarily, assess the quality of the collected walk. Without sufficient energy or engagement of the haunches, asking for half steps would be difficult. Check the rider's use of their core strength to contain the forwards impulse in the walk, and the correct application of their leg aids to ask the horse to take half steps in piaffe over the centre line.

- ❏ The purpose of half steps in piaffe is to establish the trot rhythm, in diagonal pairs. Once a few steps have been mastered, they should proceed in collected walk. Make sure both horse and rider remain relaxed throughout this exercise, as tension affects the quality of collection.

- ❏ Piaffe should be offered willingly by the horse when it is strong enough through the back to perform this advanced movement. The contact is released to demonstrate the correctness of the horse's frame, and balance.

Common faults and how to rectify these

- • If the horse is not strong enough through the back to offer piaffe, one outcome is that it comes behind the bit, dropping the contact. The resulting tense, short neck impacts on the suppleness of the back, and lowering of the haunches. Make sure the rider

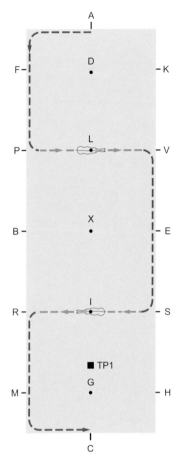

The exercise can be viewed from TP1.

is able to release the contact to demonstrate their independent seat, that is riding this movement with their seat and legs, and not over-using the reins.

- • Using the aids too firmly can impact on the activity of the hind legs. The horse receives mixed messages, with loss of rhythm, and affecting the height the legs are raised off the ground. The front feet should be raised to mid-cannon, and the hind feet to fetlock height. Ensure the rider's seat is passive enough to allow the horse's back to function, that is loins to tuck, and its lumbar back to round.

Focusing on a correct position in the saddle is important from novice to advanced level. Piaffe is pictured here.

ADVANCED JUMPING (20 × 60m ARENA)

71. REFINING JUMPING POSITION

Aims of the exercise

The aim here is to refine the rider's position and ability to improve the horse's canter in relation to jumping.

Step-by-step explanation of the exercise

Starting from A on the left rein in working canter, the rider proceeds around the arena to B, sitting in the saddle. A 20m-diameter circle is ridden, commencing at B, with half the circle ridden in a light seat (shown in blue), and the second half of the circle is ridden in jumping position (shown in green). After the circle, the rider proceeds around the arena to the small jumps at C. After jumping these, they continue around the arena to E, repeating the centre circle. A change of rein is required to ride the exercise on the right rein.

❑ Using a simple grid of three low fences tests the rider's balance, suppleness through their back and leg joints, and their independence of rein contact; that is, they are not reliant on the reins for their balance.

❑ On the circle, assess the rider's ability to turn the horse with their body, using their weight aids. This applies both when sitting in the saddle, in a light seat and in a jumping seat. Easing the horse's neck forwards with the contact, perfecting the canter seat with jumping length stirrups.

❑ Combining work in jumping position, a light forwards seat and sitting in the saddle. Ride a few strides of each, look for stability in the lower leg in all three positions. In jumping position, look for folding through the hip with arms outstretched, hips towards rear of saddle, and a flat back. In a light seat, look for balance, and flexibility through the leg joints. When sitting in the saddle, look for suppleness through the rider's back, and symmetry between both sides of the body. Assess how the rider transitions between the three seat options in canter, which will demonstrate their adaptability to the horse's needs to maintain its balance and suppleness through the back.

Common faults and how to rectify these

• Stirrup length will affect the rider's ability to do this exercise. If the stirrups are too short, this will

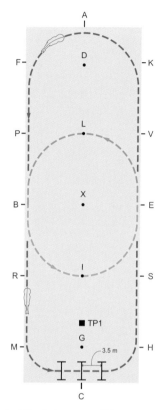

A sequence (grid) of three small jumps, or cavaletti of 0.3m in height, is set at C.

This exercise can be viewed from TP1.

impact on the rider's stability in the saddle, giving a 'perched' appearance to their seat.

• If the stirrups are too long, the security of the lower leg will be affected, impacting on the flexibility of the rider's hip and knee joints.

TOP TIP

A light forwards seat is where the rider's upper body is inclined slightly forwards. A jumping seat is where the upper body is lowered over the withers, folding at the hips, with the seat pushed towards the back of the saddle. This position puts the rider low over the horse's back as it bascules over a fence.

As the horse bascules over the fence, the rider follows the stretch through the horse's neck with their hands.
Photo courtesy of Maisie Morgan Eventing.

72. WARM-UP

Aims of the exercise

The aim here is to loosen the horse up for the demands of more advanced jumping exercises.

Step-by-step explanation of the exercise

Starting from A on the left rein in working trot rising, horse and rider proceed on the track to P. At P, they commence a 20m-diameter circle, spiralling in to a 10m-diameter circle (shown in green). They then spiral out again to the 20m-diameter circle, before continuing on the track to B. At B a change of rein is ridden to the track between S and H. This exercise can be repeated on the right rein, starting from A.

- ❑ When riding this exercise in working trot, ask the rider to focus on increasing and decreasing the bend of the horse when spiralling in and out on the circle, with the bend of the horse conforming to the size of circle.

- ❑ Once established in working trot, this exercise can be ridden in canter. When spiralling on the circle, the length of the horse's canter stride can be collected when spiralling in, and lengthened when spiralling out, in order to improve the horse's suppleness and responsive to the rider's aids.

- ❑ A change of canter lead can be made on the diagonal line, either through trot, walk or a flying change. Alternatively, the same lead can be maintained, working in counter-canter, around the short side of the arena to R, where a change of lead can be made.

- ❑ The benefits of working with the different options of lead change for jumping, or working in counter-canter, give horse and rider the confidence to be able to jump on either canter lead.

Common faults and how to rectify these

- • If the horse is tight through the back, it will be difficult for the rider to increase and decrease the amount of body-bend in the horse. This can result in the horse drifting in and out on the spiral, rather than the hind and fore feet following the same track. If this is the case, the rider should work on transitions between trot and canter around the arena before attempting the spiral again.

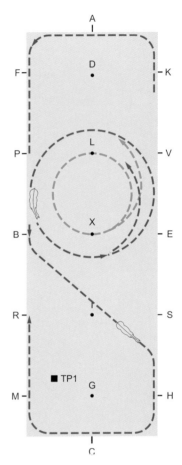

This exercise can be viewed from TP1.

- • The purpose of riding the spiral is to develop the rider's adaptability when presenting the horse to fences coming off a corner or a turn. Make sure the rider uses their weight aids correctly to spiral in and out. Leaning to one side will impact on the horse's balance.

- • Precision is required when riding out of the circle, and onto the diagonal line. Inaccuracy at B will impact on the horse's straightness for the change of lead over the centre line, and consequently affect the turn onto the track between S and H. Make sure the rider maintains a regular tempo in the canter to help the horse.

73. DIFFICULT LINES OF APPROACH

Aims of the exercise

To improve the adaptability of horse and rider when presented with challenging lines of approach.

Step-by-step explanation of the exercise

❑ Starting on the left rein from A in collected canter (left-lead), horse and rider jump the first fence, before proceeding in half pass left to fence 2, between S and H. After jumping this fence, they ride a transition to walk (shown in green), keeping the horse straight.

❑ They then pick up right-lead canter, jump fence 3, between M and R, before proceeding in half pass right to the fourth fence between V and K. Similarly, a walk transition is ridden after this fence (shown in blue), keeping the horse straight. The exercise can then be repeated from A.

❑ The value of this exercise is to help the rider to adjust the line of approach to a fence to give the horse the best chance of a successful jump. Should they turn inaccurately when jumping a course, being able to use lateral movements keeps the horse balanced while adjustment is made to the approach line.

Common faults and how to rectify these

• If the horse does not respond to the rider's sideways-driving aids in time to jump the second fence, the rider should bypass the fence, either to the inside or outside of it, and focus on the quality of the half-pass. This helps to keep the horse calm, and working in a rhythm, while the rider learns to gauge the angle required to present the horse to the centre of the fence, on the quarter line.

• By using a walk transition after jumping the second and fourth fences, the rider has the opportunity to balance the horse, and to straighten it before proceeding in right-lead canter.

• The first fence on each quarter-line must be jumped straight, with the horse flexed for half-pass after landing. This ensures a straight jump, with both hind legs taking equal weight on take-off, and subsequently landing.

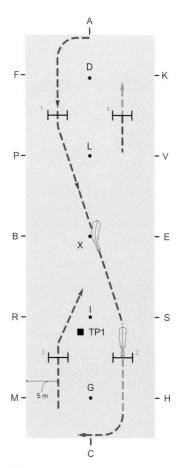

Place a small jump (0.75m in height) between F and P, so the centre of the fence is on the quarter line. Place a second fence, also on the quarter line, between M and R. On the three-quarter line, place another two fences, between S and H, and between K and V.

This exercise can be viewed from TP1.

TOP TIP

An alternative option for this exercise is to begin in counter-canter (right lead), jump fence 1, and ride leg-yield to the second fence. A change of lead to counter-canter (left lead) is required at the C end of the arena before jumping fences 3 and 4.

74. CANTER POLES WITH AN UPRIGHT FENCE

Aims of the exercise

The purpose of the canter poles is for the rider to develop a feel for the optimum canter for the horse to jump an upright fence.

Step-by-step explanation of the exercise

❏ Starting on the left rein in working canter left, the rider proceeds around the arena to S, riding a large half-circle between R and S. At S, they turn onto the diagonal line towards F; the canter stride is collected before going over the four poles and the fence. After the fence, a transition to walk is ridden, keeping the horse straight after landing (shown in green). To ride this exercise on the right rein, the poles and fence should be placed on the diagonal line RK.

❏ Make sure the rider has established a balanced collected canter around the arena before they approach the poles and fence on the diagonal. Assess the quality of the turn to their approach line, ensuring they have the horse placed in line with the centre of the poles. If the rider keeps the horse straight, with a consistent contact over the poles, and a good sense of timing, they will be able to allow the horse the freedom through the neck to bascule over the fence in balance. The walk transition after the poles is all-important, as it is the test of the ability of the horse to collect.

Common faults and how to rectify these

• If the rider struggles to maintain sufficient engagement in the horse's canter, there is a risk it may break to trot, but with the poles set at 3.5m apart there is the option for the poles to be ridden in trot, with a trot stride between the poles.

• It can also help to work on the collected canter around the arena, to make sure there is sufficient impulsion to maintain the canter stride over the poles and fence. Once this is achieved, ask the rider to try the exercise again in canter.

• If the horse tries to put a stride in between the poles, or tries to jump over two of them, the

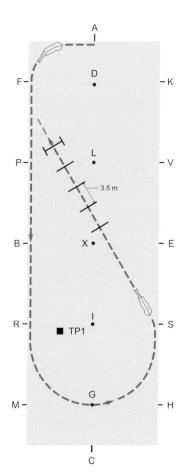

On the diagonal line SF, place four poles at 3.5m apart, followed by a small upright fence, at 0.75m in height, at a distance of 3.5m from the fourth pole.

This exercise can be viewed from TP1.

distance between the poles should be adjusted to suit the natural stride length of the horse's canter. This helps both horse and rider remain relaxed through the exercise, and to grow in confidence.

• Once the exercise is ridden successfully, the fence can be raised as required. It is important that the rider does not change the quality of the canter, or their technique when riding over a higher fence. If either horse or rider become tense, or anticipate the take-off, the fence height should be lowered, making the exercise easier.

75. CANTER POLES WITH A SPREAD FENCE

Aims of the exercise

The aim here is to regulate the canter stride on approaching a spread fence.

Step-by-step explanation of the exercise

- ❑ Starting on the left rein in working canter left, the rider approaches the line of poles, and the fence, on the quarter-line. On the approach, the canter stride should have sufficient impulsion to accommodate the distance of the spread fence. After jumping the fence, a transition to walk is ridden before reaching the track at the C end of the arena (shown in green).
- ❑ Guide the rider into establishing the optimum length of canter stride before they turn onto the approach line. It may help to do this around the arena, by riding transitions within the gait, collecting and lengthening the canter stride to generate impulsion, until the most suitable is established.
- ❑ After the fence, the rider should ride a transition back to walk as a test of their ability to collect, as well as lengthen, the stride. The exercise can be repeated.
- ❑ To ride this exercise on the right rein, the poles and fence need to be reversed, which could be done next time this exercise is ridden.

Common faults and how to rectify these

- Lengthening the canter too much, too soon, can result in a flat jump, with the risk of the horse catching a hind leg. To restore engagement, ask the rider to approach in a more collected canter, focusing on impulsion, rather than speed, on reaching the poles.
- Coming in too fast can lead to the horse breaking into trot over the poles. In this instance, make sure the rider does not anticipate the spread fence, and ride too strongly on the turn onto the fence line. The rider needs to understand that lengthening the stride should not affect the rhythm and tempo of the canter.
- If the turn is not ridden accurately, this can result in a crooked approach to the poles, which may

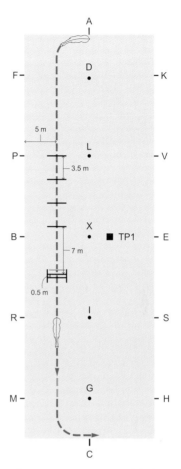

Place four poles, set at 3.5m apart, with the centre point of each on the quarter-line. The first pole should be opposite P. After the fourth pole, an ascending spread fence is placed at a distance of 7m from the fourth pole.

The exercise can be viewed from TP1.

lead to the horse running out to one side of the fence. It may help to ask the rider to ride the turn onto the approach in trot, and canter once the horse is straight.

- If the rider is unable to ride a downwards transition after the fence, they may need to work on their ability to collect the canter. The downward transition can be ridden progressively, through trot to walk to develop this.

76. DOUBLE FENCE FROM CANTER

Aims of the exercise

To perfect riding a double with one stride between the fences.

Step-by-step explanation of the exercise

❑ Starting on the left rein in working canter left, horse and rider approach the double. After jumping the fences, they proceed around the arena to C, riding a transition to walk. A change of rein can be ridden on the diagonal line MK, passing between the jumps.

❑ The skill required by the rider here is to ride an accurate turn onto the diagonal line, in order to line up the horse with the centre of the double. Ask the rider to maintain the rhythm and balance of the horse's canter on the approach and ride calmly forwards, focusing on the canter as they approach the fences. This helps the rider to feel the bascule of the horse's back when the horse takes off over the first element.

❑ Make sure they ride the non-jumping canter stride between the fences well, to give the horse the best chance of a good take-off over the second element. After the second element, they should proceed forwards in balance, around the corner at H.

❑ The walk transition at C is a test of the rider's application of their aids, and a good point to reward the horse. The change of rein across the diagonal line MK can be used to establish left-canter lead again.

❑ To jump this exercise on the right rein, the jumps should be re-positioned on the diagonal line MK, with the ground-line poles placed on the take-off side.

Common faults and how to rectify these

• If horse and rider are not lined up with the centre of the first fence, they risk jumping to one side over the fence. This has the impact of causing them to jump more to one side over the second element, with the potential of clipping one of the wings. If confidence is lost through making a mistake, the fences must be lowered to simplify the exercise.

• Riding too fast in an effort to clear both elements is another common mistake. This can result in knocking a pole from one, or both, elements.

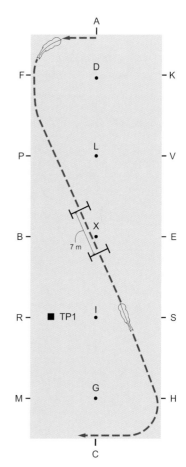

Place two simple upright fences, at a height of 0.75m, on the diagonal line FH at a distance of 7m apart, to be jumped on the left rein. Each should have a pole as a ground line on the take-off side.

This exercise can be viewed from TP1.

• A refusal can result from approaching with too little impulsion for the horse to clear both fences. It may stop before the first fence, or between the fences. To rectify this, the rider must ride positively forwards, without going too fast.

TOP TIP

The fences can be varied by using an ascending spread fence as the second element, or a parallel.

77. BOUNCE FENCE

Aims of the exercise

To develop riding a bounce fence with three elements to improve co-ordination and dexterity of both horse and rider.

Step-by-step explanation of the exercise

Place three small fences, at a height of no more than 0.75m and 3.5m apart, on the quarter line. Each should have a pole as a ground line on the take-off side.

❑ Starting on the left rein in collected canter, horse and rider approach the bounce fences in left lead canter. After jumping, they proceed straight on the quarter line, riding a walk transition before reaching the short side (shown in green). After a few walk steps, they proceed in collected canter around the arena, to repeat the exercise.

❑ Look for the rider turning accurately onto the line of approach, and the straightness of the horse on the quarter line. Check the rider's ability to fold through the hips over each element. They should be flexible through their hip, knee and ankle joints in order to accommodate the movement of the horse's back as it jumps, bearing in mind there is no non-jumping stride between the elements.

❑ Check they maintain a supportive contact, following the movement of the horse's neck as it jumps. After the third element, the rider should sit in the saddle, using half-halts to bring the horse back to walk, as a test of control and balance. This is a good point to praise the horse before resuming canter to repeat the exercise.

❑ To jump this exercise on the right rein, move the ground-line poles to the take-off side of each fence.

Common faults and how to rectify these

• Coming in too fast disturbs the rhythm of the canter, making it difficult for the horse to maintain its canter stride. To rectify this, the rider must maintain a balanced canter, with sufficient impulsion to clear all three elements.

• If the approach is not straight there is a risk the horse will drift to one side. This affects the distance between the fences, making each longer and more effort for the horse. It may help to

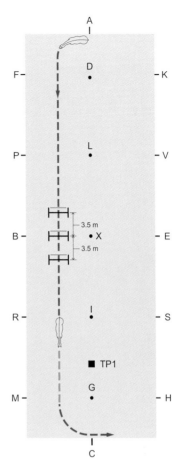

Place three small fences, at a height of no more than 0.75m, on the quarter line. Each should have a pole as a ground line on the take-off side.

This exercise can be viewed from TP1.

ask the rider to focus on a point at the C end of the arena, once they are lined up with the first element, to help to keep the horse straight.

• If the walk transition after the fences is difficult to achieve, make sure the contact is correct when jumping. Taking too strong a hold can cause the horse to pull, affecting the engagement of the haunches. If the contact is dropped, the horse may run forwards, or veer to one side. In both cases, if the rider is confident, putting both reins into one hand can help them focus on having regard for the horse's mouth, and riding with their body.

78. TWO-STRIDE DOUBLE

Aims of the exercise

The aim here is to improve the technique of horse and rider when riding a double with two non-jumping strides.

Step-by-step explanation of the exercise

❑ Starting on the left rein, in working canter, left lead, horse and rider jump the double. After the second element, keeping the horse straight, a walk transition is ridden before reaching the track at H. Horse and rider then proceed in working canter around the arena, changing the rein on the diagonal MK to repeat the exercise.

❑ When jumping a double with two non-jumping strides, the rider needs to focus on the strides between the fences – that is, the consistency of the canter throughout this exercise. The rider needs to ride the canter with sufficient impulsion to ensure the horse clears the fences, but also requires to keep control in order to collect the horse after the second element for the walk transition.

❑ As the rider becomes more skilled, they will develop the ability to adjust the stride length accordingly, so if the horse takes off too far away from the first element, the rider can ride the non-jumping strides bigger to compensate. Conversely, if the horse takes off too close to the first element, the non-jumping strides can be made bigger.

❑ To ride this exercise on the right rein, the double is constructed on the diagonal line MK.

Common faults and how to rectify these

• Straightness can be an issue with jumping a double with two non-jumping strides, as the distance between the fences increases the margin of error. The rider needs to ride the turn onto the approach line accurately, otherwise the horse may drift to one side between the fences, making taking off over the second element difficult.

• Coming with too little impulsion runs the risk of the horse not having sufficient energy to jump the second element, resulting in a refusal or a run-out.

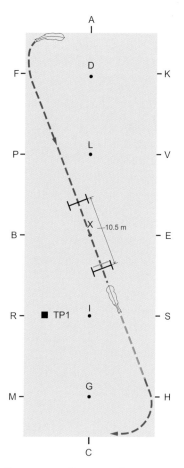

Place two fences at a distance of 10.5m apart, on the diagonal line FH, to give two non-jumping strides. The first element can be an upright fence, and the second an ascending spread. Their height should not exceed 0.75m.

This exercise can be viewed from TP1.

Make sure the horse and rider maintain a good quality of canter throughout this exercise.

• Approaching with too much speed can put the horse on its forehand, making it difficult to have enough spring in the canter to clear the fences, so risking knocking them. In this instance, ask the rider to come in at a steadier pace. The walk transition after the fences is an important test of the canter being ridden at the correct speed, and in good balance.

79. JUMPING GRID

Aims of the exercise

To improve the co-ordination and dexterity of both the horse and rider when jumping a line of fences in a grid.

Step-by-step explanation of the exercise

❑ Starting from A on the left rein in collected canter, horse and rider approach the grid in left lead canter. After completing the grid, a walk transition is ridden before reaching the track at H, before proceeding again in canter. A change of rein is required on the diagonal line MK to repeat this exercise.

❑ The rider must keep the horse straight, in line with the centre of each element, to successfully complete the grid. The quality of the canter is key, so make sure the rider only approaches the fences when they have the horse absolutely in balance and control. Being able to maintain consistency in their riding technique when jumping multiple fences takes skill. If all these aspects are correct, the rider will be able to bring the horse to walk after the last element with ease.

❑ To ride this exercise on the right rein, the grid should be reconstructed on the diagonal line MK, which could be done the next time this exercise is ridden.

Common faults and how to rectify these

• Riding forwards in a consistent canter throughout the grid avoids the issue of loss of impulsion, which can affect the quality of jumping, in that the horse may knock the fences. Make sure, though, that the rider does not confuse forwardness with speed, as coming into the grid too fast can cause major issues with jumping quality.

• Drifting to one side, even slightly, can lead to the horse and rider jumping close to the jump wings by the end of the grid. If the rider's chosen line of approach is even slightly off centre, they should be asked to turn the horse away and make a fresh attempt. Ensure they are not too close to the first element when they do this, as this could lead to a refusal on the next approach.

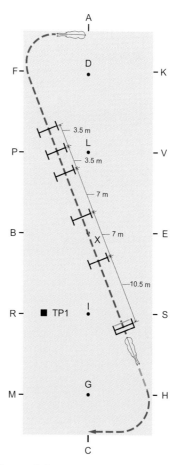

On the diagonal line FH, place three small bounce fences at a distance of 3.5m apart. These are followed by two fences at a distance of 7m, with the final element at a distance of 10.5m, to give two non-jumping strides. The height of the fences should not exceed 0.75m. The fences can be constructed as simple upright fences, with the last element an ascending spread.

This exercise can be viewed from TP1.

• When riding the walk transition after the last element, there is a risk the rider may begin thinking about this too soon, causing the horse to back off the last element. To rectify this, make sure the rider rides the horse forwards to the end of the grid, while still maintaining control and balance to bring the horse back to walk after landing.

TOP TIP

Working on collecting and extending the canter stride can help with jumping a grid (see Exercise 62).

80. WHOLE COURSE IN CANTER

Aims of the exercise

The aim here is to consolidate previous jumping experience into riding a whole course.

Step-by-step explanation of the exercise

❑ Starting from A on the left rein, horse and rider approach fence 1, inclining left to jump fence 2. After fence 2, a change of canter lead is required to jump fence 3, changing lead again before approaching fence 4, the double.

❑ In left lead canter, they approach fence 5, before turning onto the approach line for fence 6, the double with two non-jumping strides. There is a longer gap between this double and fence 7 to give the horse and rider a chance to relax into their stride. After fence 7, there is a straight approach to fence 8, the final fence.

❑ Before jumping the course as a whole, it can help horse and rider to familiarise themselves with the elements of the course by jumping two related fences at a time. This can highlight any potential difficulties that may arise.

Common faults and how to rectify these

• The ability to maintain the quality of the canter is key to successfully jumping a course. Being able to collect and extend the stride is important in order for the rider to present the horse to each fence accurately to ensure a clean jump.

• Should a poor approach be made to a fence, ask them to turn away and try again. Make sure this is done tactfully and the horse is not turned too sharply away from a fence, as this can lead to a refusal the next time.

• If jumping a particular fence could be improved upon, the rider can be asked to try again before continuing with the rest of the course. If time is spent on this, check that neither horse nor rider is becoming tired. If this is the case, the exercise should be brought to an end, and the course jumped another day. It is so important to end on a good note, so both horse and rider take something positive from their session.

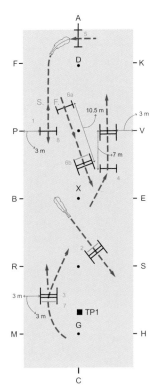

A course of fences is constructed, with fence 1 – a simple upright – 3m in from the track opposite P, to be jumped from both directions, as this is also fence 8. Fence 2, an ascending spread, is jumped towards H. Fence 3 (also fence 7), between M and R, is a spread fence to be jumped on the right rein. Fence 4 is a double with one non-jumping stride, the first element an upright, and the second a parallel. Fence 5 is situated on the track at A, jumped on the left rein, followed by fence 6, a double with two non-jumping strides, the second element an ascending spread. Fence 7 is followed by fence 8 to complete the course. (The start and finish points are indicated in blue.)

The course can be viewed from TP1.

A confident partnership when riding cross country is important to build trust and improve ability.
Photo courtesy of Maisie Morgan Eventing.

ADVANCED PROPS (20 × 60m ARENA)

81. USING DRESSAGE LETTERS: IMPROVING LATERAL WORK

Aims of the exercise

The aim here is to use the arena dressage letters accurately when riding half-pass and shoulder-in, when to bend or straighten the horse, and to perfect transitions between these lateral movements.

Step-by-step explanation of the exercise

Starting from A on the left rein in collected walk, shoulder-in is ridden from F to P (shown in green). From P, half-pass left is ridden across the arena to S (shown in blue). From S to M, the horse is ridden straight. On the right rein, shoulder-in is ridden from M to R (shown in green), with half-pass right ridden across the arena to V (shown in blue). The horse is then ridden straight around the arena to F in order to repeat the exercise.

❏ When shoulder-in is ridden, F to P, and M to R, check the alignment of the rider's upper body to the shoulder position of the horse. Also, ensure the shoulder-in is ridden on three tracks. It may help to change the point of observation to TP2 to view the shoulder-in head-on on either rein.

❏ To ride the transition into half-pass, if the angle of the shoulder-in is correct, the rider should commence half-pass as the horse's head comes into alignment with the diagonal line, PS or RV. At the end of the diagonal line, where horse and rider approach the track at S or V, the bend of the horse should be maintained until its head reaches the track, at which point the rider should straighten the horse.

❏ This exercise can also be ridden in collected trot and canter. In canter, counter-canter can be ridden on the track following the half-pass, from S to H, and from V to K, before making a change of lead through walk, trot, or a flying change at K or H.

Common faults and how to rectify these

• Asking for too much neck bend, both in the shoulder-in and half-pass, can cause the horse to fall out through the shoulder. Though the rider may be maintaining the same bend in both movements, if the amount of neck bend is excessive

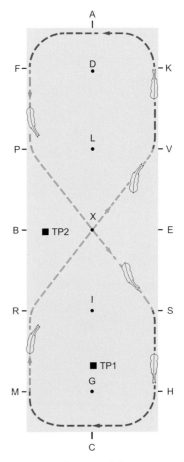

This exercise can be viewed from TP1 and TP2.

the horse will be unbalanced. To rectify this fault, ask the rider to view the horse's neck position from above, making sure the horse's nose is no further to the inside than the point of its inside shoulder.

• Observing the rider's seat is important to monitor their consistency of weight in the saddle. While putting weight into the inside stirrup is advisable, overloading the inside seat bone inhibits the horse's ability to step under behind in the direction of travel.

• If there is a difference between the suppleness of the horse to the left and right, make sure the rider's aids are consistent in both directions.

Checking the rider's position frequently during a lesson helps to develop muscle memory.

82. CONES FOR TRANSITIONS

Aims of the exercise

The aim here is to improve straightness when riding direct transitions and flying changes.

Step-by-step explanation of the exercise

❑ Starting from A on the left rein in collected trot, the rider proceeds on the diagonal line FE. Between the cones at L, they ride a direct transition to halt. Proceeding in collected trot, they turn onto the diagonal line EM, riding a direct transition to halt between the cones at I.

❑ When direct transitions are ridden between each pair of cones, the correct timing is when the rider's knees are in line with the cones. Make sure the rider prepares the horse with half-halts before riding a direct transition. The halt should be square, and the horse's outline consistent. On proceeding in collected trot after the halt transition, make sure the rider keeps the horse straight on the diagonal lines FE and EM.

❑ An important point in this exercise is to ride a balanced turn at E onto the diagonal line EM. A good turn here ensures the horse is straight, and in line with the cones at I.

❑ When riding this exercise in canter, a change of lead through walk can be made between each pair of cones, making sure the rider collects the canter sufficiently to maintain the horse's engagement of its haunches in both the downward and upward transitions. This ensures the quality of both the walk and the canter.

❑ Another alternative is for a flying change to be ridden between each pair of cones.

Common faults and how to rectify these

• Often, transitions are mistimed, being executed when the horse's head comes in line with the designated marker. Make sure it is the rider that lines up with the cones.

• If horse and rider have difficulty in maintaining balance in trot on the turn between the diagonals at E, it can be ridden in walk.

• When riding this exercise in canter, a transition to walk, before reaching E, can help to re-balance

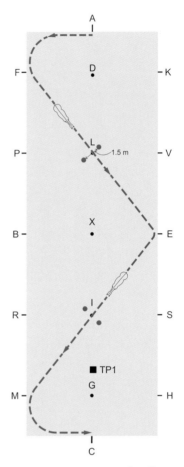

Place two cones, 1.5m apart, on the diagonal line FE, either side of L. Place a second pair, 1.5m apart, on the diagonal line EM, either side of I.

This exercise can be viewed from TP1.

the horse. Pick up canter again once the rider has the horse lined up with the cones on the diagonal EM.

• If the horse drifts to one side when executing a flying change, there is a risk they will get too close to one of the cones, or miss them altogether. If this happens, ask the rider to change the canter lead through walk instead between the cones. Once successful, the flying changes can be resumed.

83. CONES FOR CIRCLES (10m DIAMETER)

Aims of the exercise

The aim here is to ride perfect 10m-diameter circles in both directions, changing the rein from one circle to another.

Step-by-step explanation of the exercise

❑ Starting from A on the left rein in medium walk, a 10m-diameter circle (shown in red) is ridden around cone 1, opposite B. A second 10m-diameter circle (shown in green) is ridden around cone 2. On crossing the centre line on the second half of this circle, a third circle (shown in blue) is ridden to the right around cone 5. The rider returns to the circle around cone 2, on the left rein.

❑ This sequence of circles is repeated around cones 3 and 4, on the left rein, and a circle right around cone 6.

❑ A change of rein is required to ride this exercise on the right rein, connecting with a circle right around cone 3.

❑ Make sure the right amount of flexion and bend is established before commencing the first circle at B. This helps the rider to judge the size and shape of the circle around the cone. Check their accuracy when changing bend to ride the circle right (shown in blue) around cone 5, and when returning to the circle left (shown in green). After this circle, they again proceed around the perimeter of the cones to the next 10m-diameter circle around cone 3, and so on.

❑ This exercise can be ridden in collected trot.

❑ If attempting this exercise in canter, be aware that it requires a confident horse and rider, and an established ability to collect. A simple change of lead through walk is required for the small figure of eight around cones 2 and 5 (and repeated around cones 4 and 6).

Common faults and how to rectify these

• Inconsistency of circle size is highlighted by riding around the cones. To improve accuracy, make sure they ride the horse the same distance from each cone on every circle.

• When riding the small figures of eight (green and

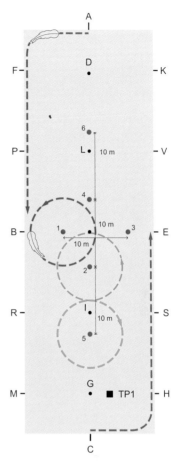

Six cones are required for this exercise. Four are equally spaced on the centre line, at a distance of 10m apart, with X being the centre point of the middle two cones. Two more cones are placed on the BE line, each being 10m away from X.

This exercise can be viewed from TP1.

blue circles) the rider must take care to change the flexion and bend of the horse exactly between the two cones. If they are off centre, the circles will be of different sizes.

• If horse and rider have difficulty with the circles being ridden in quick succession, ask them to omit the circles around cones 1 and 3, and focus on the small figures of eight (green and blue circles).

84. CONES FOR ZIGZAGS

Aims of the exercise

The aim here is to improve accuracy, when riding half-pass zigzags.

Step-by-step explanation of the exercise

❑ Starting on the left rein in collected walk, horse and rider turn onto the centre line at A. Half-pass left is ridden from D to the outside of the cone at V. From this point, half-pass right is ridden to the outside of the cone opposite R, with its centre point passing through X. Half-pass left is then ridden to the centre line at G, where horse and rider proceed straight to C, turning right onto the track. They then continue straight on the long side back to A in order to repeat the exercise on the right rein.

❑ Check the turn onto the centre line at A is accurate, and that the rider positions the horse in preparation for half-pass left. Half-halts should be used to balance the horse as a change of bend is ridden just before establishing the new bend for half-pass right around the first cone. Similar preparation is required for the last half-pass back to the centre line. Make sure the rider straightens the horse at G before turning right at C.

❑ This exercise can be ridden in trot and canter. When riding it in canter, a flying change is required when changing direction. In this event, it is important that the rider positions the horse accurately for each change to ensure they are clean, and the bend is correct for the half-pass in the new direction.

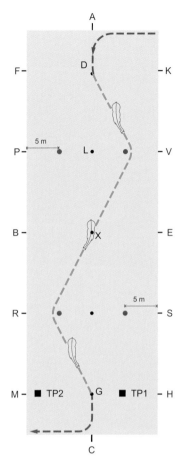

Four cones are required for this exercise. Place one on the quarter line 5m in from the track opposite P, and a second 5m in from the track at R. On the other side of the arena, place two more cones, one 5m in from the track at S, and the last opposite V.

This exercise can be viewed from TP1 when ridden on the left rein, and TP2 when ridden on the right rein.

Common faults and how to rectify these

- If horse and rider have difficulty executing a change of bend around the cones, they could add a 10m-diameter circle to give them time to establish the new bend before proceeding in half-pass.

- If the forwardness of the horse is lost, the middle section of the zigzag can be ridden straight, in order to increase the horse's impulsion. The rider will need to collect the horse again before riding half-pass left for the second time.

- If this exercise is ridden in canter, the rider should take care that sufficient room is given around each cone to ride a flying change. Failure to do so could result in the horse clipping a cone.

85. POLES FOR TRAVERS

Aims of the exercise

To improve straightness between changes of bend in travers.

Step-by-step explanation of the exercise

❑ Starting from A in collected walk on the left rein, horse and rider turn onto the centre line. From D to L, they ride in travers, with the haunches left, to the first pair of poles, where they straighten the horse (shown in green). They then change bend, with the haunches right, to the second pair of poles, where the horse is straightened (shown in green). They proceed to G in travers left, ride straight to C, and track left to repeat the exercise.

❑ A change of rein is required to repeat the exercise on the right rein.

❑ First, ensure the rider turns the horse accurately on the centre line. When riding travers in each direction, it can be helpful for the rider to have in mind keeping the horse's ears in line with the centre line to keep between the poles. They can then focus on positioning the horse's body to bring it into travers. It can be helpful when positioning the horse if the rider remembers to maintain the same bend in travers as is required for a 10m-diameter circle.

❑ This exercise can be ridden in trot, but ensure the rider uses half-halts to maintain the horse's engagement and balance throughout the exercise.

❑ If this exercise is ridden in canter, a change of canter lead through walk will be required between each pair of poles to maintain collection. Left-lead canter is required for travers left, and right-lead canter for travers right.

Common faults and how to rectify these

• If the haunches are moved too far over, with too strong an outside leg aid, the three-track position of travers will be lost, and the horse will drift sideways rather than remain in balance.

• Planning ahead is required at the end of the centre line to straighten the horse after riding the last travers to G. Riders can find this the most difficult part of riding lateral movements on the centre line, as the turn onto the track at C follows quickly.

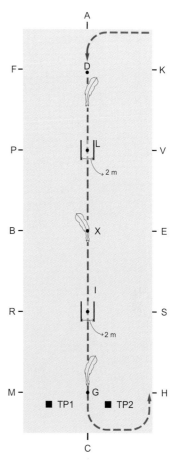

Two pairs of parallel poles are required, set at 2m apart, placed on the centre line. The first pair are placed with L as their centre point, and the second at I.

This exercise can be viewed from TP1 when ridden on the left rein, and TP2 on the right rein.

• There can be confusion with the positioning of the horse's shoulders in travers. A simple tip is to ask for bend through the horse's whole body, as on a 10m-diameter circle.

TOP TIP

As this exercise is ridden on the centre line, the movement is described here as travers right, and travers left. When riding this exercise on the long side of the arena, it would be described as riding travers (haunches-in) and renvers (haunches-out).

86. POLES FOR CHANGES OF REIN (DIRECTION)

Aims of the exercise

This exercise focuses on precision at either end of diagonal lines when changing the rein.

Step-by-step explanation of the exercise

❑ Starting from A in medium walk, the horse and rider turn onto the diagonal PS, passing between the poles. After S, they continue around the arena to R, riding on the diagonal to V. They then proceed around the arena to A to repeat the exercise.

❑ The placement of the poles brings the rider's attention to positioning the horse accurately at both ends of the diagonal, when leaving and re-joining the track.

❑ As they leave the track at P, when the rider's outside knee is level with the letter, they position the horse to the left. As they reach the first pair of poles, check the horse is absolutely straight before proceeding. They ride through the pair of poles before S, after which the rider positions the horse to the right, to prepare for turning right onto the track.

❑ Proceeding on the right rein to R, they ride through the both pairs of poles on the diagonal to V, positioning the horse to the right before the first pair, and to the left after the second pair.

❑ When riding this exercise in trot, the poles are useful to help the rider straighten the horse before riding a transition to medium trot, at P and R, and riding a transition back to working, or collected, trot between the poles at S and V.

❑ When riding the exercise in canter, transitions can be made between the poles into, and out of, medium canter. Another option is to ride a flying change between the poles at the ends of the diagonals at S and V.

Common faults and how to rectify these

• If the horse drifts to one side across the diagonal, make sure the rider is sitting straight in the saddle, with an even rein contact. Ask them to correct this before they reach the poles at the end of each diagonal. If necessary, they can halt at X to make corrections to their position.

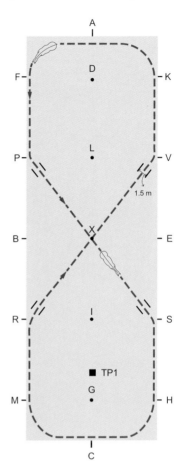

Place a pair of parallel poles, set at 1.5m apart, at either end of the diagonal lines PS and RV.

This exercise can be viewed from TP1.

• If the horse is not placed so it is looking in the direction of travel, there is a risk of over-shooting the poles when turning onto the diagonal. If this happens, horse and rider can continue around the track and start again.

TOP TIP

Lining the horse's ears up with the diagonal line before turning helps the rider to judge the turn. Similarly, lining its ears up with the track before turning onto it at the end of the diagonal helps them to judge when to ride the turn onto the track. The rider should look between the horse's ears.

87. POLES FOR FOUR-LOOP SERPENTINES

Aims of the exercise

The aim here is to perfect riding a four-loop serpentine.

Step-by-step explanation of the exercise

❏ Starting from A on the left rein in medium walk, a four-loop serpentine is ridden, passing between the three pairs of poles on the centre line. The exercise can be repeated on the right rein, commencing from C.

❏ The rider should position the horse correctly for each loop of the serpentine, looking in the direction of travel. Each loop should be the same shape and size, with one stride on the track, while maintaining flexion and bend in the direction of travel.

❏ When riding this exercise in walk, or trot, a transition to halt can be ridden between the poles before riding forwards again. This moment can be useful to check the straightness of horse and rider, the horse's outline, and the rider's position.

❏ Transitions within the gait, such as riding the serpentine in medium walk, or working trot, with collected strides ridden between the poles, can be added to develop the horse's engagement of its haunches.

❏ When riding this exercise in canter, a change of lead can be ridden between the poles, either through trot or walk. The rider should aim for 3–4 steps of walk or trot between the poles to allow time to change flexion and bend before and after the transition.

❏ Another option is to ride a flying change between the poles, keeping the horse straight for the change of lead.

Common faults and how to rectify these

• Instead of looking in the direction of travel, a common mistake is for the rider to turn their head too much in an effort to turn the horse, rather than their using their upper body. Make sure their hips and shoulders are in alignment with the horse throughout the exercise.

• If the horse overshoots the loops, ask the rider to ride a 15m-diameter circle, to improve the shape of the loop, before crossing the centre line through the poles.

• If the horse is not ridden exactly in the centre of each pair of poles, straightness across the centre line is lost. This has a knock-on effect on the shape

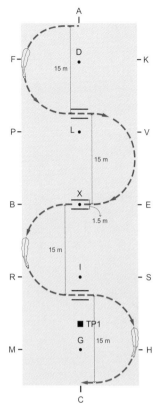

Three pairs of parallel poles, set at 1.5m apart are required, placed across the centre line at a distance of 15m from each end of the arena, and each other.

This exercise can be viewed from TP1.

of the following loop, with the horse falling out, making it too large, or falling in, making it too small. To rectify this, check the rider is using their inside and outside leg aids correctly.

A sense of achievement is as important for the horse as it is for the rider.

88. POLES FOR REIN-BACK

Aims of the exercise

The aim here is to improve the technique for rein-back.

Step-by-step explanation of the exercise

❏ Starting from A on the left rein in medium walk, horse and rider proceed around the arena to B, passing alongside the poles. A transition to halt is ridden at the furthest point between the second pair of poles (indicated in blue) before riding rein-back (shown in green).

❏ On proceeding around the arena in medium walk, they turn onto the centre line at C, riding a transition to halt at the furthest point between the second pair of poles (indicated in blue) before riding rein-back (shown in green).

❏ They then proceed in medium walk on the centre line, turning right at A. Halt and rein-back are repeated between the poles opposite E.

❏ Riding a halt transition between the poles before commencing rein-back gives the opportunity to make sure the horse is in a correct outline, with its haunches engaged.

❏ Check the horse's leg sequence of diagonal pairs in rein-back is clear. Make sure the rider eases the contact, to ensure they are not using too strong a rein when asking the horse to go backwards.

❏ Another option is to repeat the rein-back before proceeding, riding it twice, which is a great test of the rider's technique.

❏ When riding this exercise in trot, make sure the rider collects the horse with half-halts, as preparation for the preceding halt to the rein-back.

Common faults and how to rectify these

• Halting too far after the poles leaves room for crookedness in the rein-back, risking stepping to one side of the poles, knocking them, or even stepping on them, so it is important the rider halts with the horse's haunches between the poles.

• If the halt is asked for too early, before the horse's haunches are within the poles, this can also result

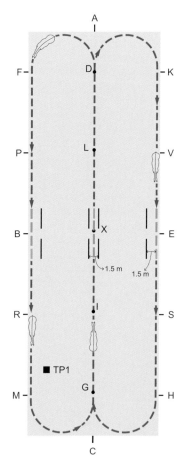

Two pairs of poles are placed, end to end, opposite B and 1.5m in from the track. Similarly, two pairs of poles are positioned opposite E. On the centre line, two pairs of poles are placed end to end at a distance of 1.5m from each other, with their centre point being X.

This exercise can be viewed from TP1.

in drifting to one side in the rein-back. The rider should be able to correct this with correct use of their leg aids.

• Care should be taken to ride straight on the centre line, lining the horse up with the middle of the poles. If a poor turn at C is ridden, the rider leaves themselves a lot to do in the way of straightening the horse, before riding the rein-back.

89. COMBINATION PROPS FOR ACCURACY

Aims of the exercise

The aim here is to combine the use of poles and cones to improve accuracy when riding advanced movements.

Step-by-step explanation of the exercise

❑ Starting from A in medium walk, horse and rider ride around the corner cone and proceed to F, riding half-pass left to X (indicated in green). On reaching X, a 10m-diameter circle right is executed (shown in blue). On returning to X, half-pass right is ridden to M, passing around the cone in the corner.

❑ Turning onto the centre line between the poles at G, horse and rider proceed to X, halting between the cones. They then proceed on the centre line to D, passing between the poles at D before turning right onto the track at A. The exercise can then be repeated on the right rein.

❑ The placement of the cones in the corners, and on the centre line, is to draw the rider's attention to the bend of the horse through the corners, the half-pass in each direction, and the 10m-diameter circle. The poles either side of the centre line are placed with the aim of guiding horse and rider onto, and away from, the centre line, as required in dressage tests.

❑ The centre line can either be ridden with the horse straight, or used for shoulder-in or travers, with a change of bend between the cones either side of X.

❑ In canter, this exercise will require a change of canter lead at X, between the cones before commencing the 10m-diameter circle. This can be through walk, trot, or a flying change.

Common faults and how to rectify these

• This exercise helps to highlight any inconsistency in the scales of training, that is rhythm, suppleness, contact, impulsion, straightness and collection. If any difficulties arise, the rider should be encouraged to pay close attention to the horse's way of going, its relaxation and enjoyment of the training process.

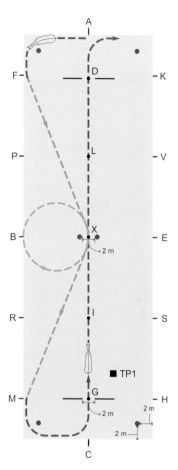

A cone is placed in each corner of the arena, at a distance of 2m from the sides. A further two cones are placed either side of the centre line at X, also at 2m apart. Two poles are positioned either side of the centre line at D, leaving a gap of 2m between them. Similarly, two poles are positioned either side of G.

This exercise can be viewed from TP1.

• Lack of preparation for any of the movements here will affect their execution. Check for the rider's use of half-halts in preparation for any part of this combination exercise, and their understanding of positioning the horse, that is flexion and bend.

• Any part of the exercise can be repeated, in isolation, if necessary, to ensure good technique, before riding the whole exercise with fluency.

90. COMBINATION PROPS FOR COLLECTION AND EXTENSION

Aims of the exercise

The aim of the exercise is to combine poles and cones to help the horse and rider develop collection and extension within the gaits.

Step-by-step explanation of the exercise

- ❑ Starting from A on the left rein in medium walk, horse and rider proceed around the arena to B. At B, ask the rider to ride a 20m-diameter circle around the outside of the four poles, with a transition within the gait as their shoulders come parallel with each pole. Each segment of the circle is ridden in a different walk. The first transition, to collected walk, is ridden by the pole on the centre line opposite I. This can be followed by a transition to medium walk at the next pole, opposite E, and extended walk for the last segment, returning to B.

- ❑ On returning to B, they proceed around the arena to H, turning onto the diagonal line HF (indicated in blue), passing between the cones at either end, to change the rein.

- ❑ Proceeding on the track to A, the exercise is repeated, riding a circle around the outside of the poles on the right rein, commencing at E (shown in green). The transitions within the walk can be repeated.

- ❑ A change of rein is ridden from M to K (shown in blue), passing between the cones at either end of this diagonal line.

- ❑ When riding this exercise in trot, transitions between collected, working and medium trot can be ridden at each pole, with extended trot ridden on the diagonals.

- ❑ In canter, collected, working and medium canter can be ridden around the poles, with extended canter ridden on the diagonals.

Common faults and how to rectify these

- • This exercise helps to highlight any inconsistency in the scales of training, that is rhythm, suppleness, contact, impulsion, straightness and collection. If any difficulties arise, the rider should be encouraged to pay close attention to the horse's

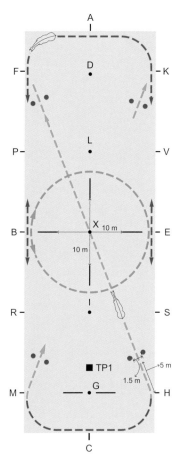

Four poles are arranged in a star formation around X, with their inner edges 10m apart. A total of eight cones are placed in pairs, 1.5m apart, situated either end of the diagonal lines FH and MK. Each pair of cones should be placed 5m in from the ends of each diagonal line.

This exercise can be viewed from TP1.

way of going, its relaxation and enjoyment of the training process.

- • Lack of preparation for any of the movements here will affect their execution. Check for the rider's use of half-halts in preparation for any part of this combination exercise, and their understanding of transitions, both within the gaits, and from one gait to another.

- • Any part of the exercise can be repeated, in isolation, if necessary, to ensure good technique, before riding the whole exercise with fluency.

WHAT MAKES A GOOD TEACHER: GUIDELINES FOR TEACHING TECHNIQUE

91. TEACHING PHILOSOPHY

Aims of the exercise

To be successful, a teacher requires a clear under-standing of their values, beliefs and ambition in that role. This exercise aims to help you evaluate what gives you fulfilment when teaching.

Explanation of teaching philosophy

'Teaching philosophy' is about the teacher's personal goal, as a teacher. In order to feel confident, and fulfilled, as a teacher, the lessons delivered must suit your values and beliefs.

❑ To a teacher, teaching may be seen as the transference of skills from teacher to student. What students learn from you can be life-long learning for them, transforming them into capable and considerate riders. This is no mean feat, and a great responsibility for you.

❑ One aspect to consider is how you view your role. Would you describe yourself as a coach, an instructor, a mentor? Each lesson may require aspects of all of these, by encouraging self-development, giving information, explanation and support.

❑ You could ask yourself how best teaching skills are put to use: are you proficient at teaching groups or individuals, and does the style of lesson give you a sense of satisfaction?

❑ Teaching in a way that sits comfortably with your beliefs leads to a sense of enjoyment and pleasure in seeing pupils develop as riders, and as individuals.

❑ Using your own expertise – and riding experience – to inform your teaching, for example passing on your own passion for dressage, can bring a sense of fulfilment and pride to you and your pupils.

❑ Growth as a teacher occurs through years of teaching, and your philosophy can change over time, indicating professional growth.

Common faults and how to rectify these

• A passionate teacher will happily teach for hours, but maintaining a level of passion and engagement with pupils can easily fade through overwork. To avoid 'burnout', a reasonable work schedule should be put in place, taking advantage of quiet times. Coping

Teaching Philosophy	Strengths	Weaknesses	Areas to improve
Teaching role			
Expertise			
Passion			
Sense of Fulfilment			

Using the self-assessment table, assess your own teaching philosophy: how you see yourself as a teacher, your area of expertise, where your passion lies, and what gives you a sense of fulfilment as a teacher.

with cancellations, resulting in a loss of income, can be stressful, but using this time in a beneficial way, to rest and recuperate, can restore life balance. Having other interests can be restorative, as can be spending time on your own riding, and training.

• Pupils that do not share your passion in a lesson can be demoralising, affecting your motivation. In this situation a strategy could be to lessen expectations of the session outcome, to ensure the session ends on a good note, for both you and your pupil.

• Should a client want to work on something in a lesson that you do not feel is appropriate, an exercise that is a stepping stone could be used, with the aim of achieving a satisfactory outcome for both.

Building the rider's confidence by establishing a rapport between them and the horse.

92. SHARING EXPERIENCE

Aims of the exercise

This exercise aims to differentiate between the useful sharing of the teacher's and the student's experience, and when it could add value, or be detrimental to the rider's progress.

Explanation of sharing experience

Teachers may give information about their riding experience with the aim of instilling confidence in the rider as to their ability and expertise. But being a successful equestrian competitor does not necessarily lead to becoming a good teacher, so teaching skills are essential. A good teacher should be informed by their personal experience, but keep the focus of the lesson on the requirements of the rider and their horse.

- ❏ Sufficient time should be allowed in each lesson for the rider to ask questions, and for you to clarify points that arise. Talking time can give horse and rider a rest from an exercise, or used as a break between different exercises.

- ❏ The teacher themselves must be trained in what they impart to others, be it sharing knowledge, instructions and support. You should have sufficient depth of knowledge to be able to answer the rider's questions. Answers should be helpful and concise in order to add value to the lesson.

- ❏ A student may want to talk through prior experience in a lesson, particularly if it caused them to be fearful or anxious. In this case, it is helpful to listen, and not to judge. It is useful to bear in mind that the teacher can learn from the student, so their experience can be informative to the teaching method employed.

Common faults and how to rectify these

- • Students will feel undermined by hearing details of your experiences. Long-winded explanations, and going off the point, will distract the rider from the exercise in hand. Share expertise only

Sharing Experience	Benefit	Detriment	Considerations
Experience as a rider			
Experience as a teacher			
Student's positive experience			
Student's negative experience			
General observations			

Using the self-assessment table, evaluate your views on sharing experience between you and your students.

when it is in the students' best interests. The regaling of long stories of past victories should be avoided during the lesson, and saved for a more appropriate opportunity.

- • There are many differing opinions in the equestrian industry, and these have no place in a riding lesson. A teacher should keep their opinions to themselves when teaching, though discussion could be invited afterwards.

- • Sharing stories about other students is a breach of confidentiality, and should be avoided. This may also send alarm bells to the student, as to whether their teacher is going to tell others about their progress – particularly failure – which could undermine their confidence.

However, sharing general observations can be useful to give the rider encouragement, and reassurance, should they experience self-doubt and a loss of confidence when having difficulty with an exercise.

93. TEACHER ATTRIBUTES

Aims of the exercise

The aim here is to consider the attributes of a good teacher. Being able to critically evaluate your own strengths and weaknesses as a teacher leads to growth, and professional development.

Explanation of what attributes make a good teacher

Having personal experience of being a student will inform you of what student expectations might be in lessons, with reference to both positive and negative experiences.

❑ Patience is essential for the teacher. Both horse and rider need time to absorb information, and to carry out instructions. Therefore, repetition is key to learning, establishing neural pathways in the brain and physical skills, by means of muscle memory.

❑ When planning a lesson, or series of lessons, for horse and rider, consider the outcome of each session. Based upon the exercises used, and why, bear in mind what you see as important for the rider to learn, and what their focus will be. Think through what you are hoping the rider can achieve, and how to deliver the session.

❑ Observational skills require focus and concentration, so as not to miss vital clues from horse and rider, informing you if your student is understanding the lesson and improving, or having difficulty and needing help and support.

❑ An important attribute for a teacher is to seek their own support, by undertaking Continuing Professional Development (CPD) or by sharing experiences with peers. The equestrian industry is tough, so a supportive network of family and friends is valuable in retaining life balance.

Common faults and how to rectify these

• Frustration can seep in, on behalf of both the teacher and rider, if a student does not understand what is expected from them. Finding an alternative way of putting things across is essential to maintain their confidence and give them a sense of achievement.

Teaching Attributes	Strengths	Weaknesses	Areas to improve
Personal experience of being a student			
Patience			
Planning			
Observation			
Empathy			
Communication			
Resistance			
Support			

Using the self-assessment table, evaluate your attributes as a teacher.

• Good communication is essential. Language should be used that the rider understands, without being condescending, or 'blinding them with science'. More experienced riders will understand equestrian terminology, but the overuse of 'jargon' with a novice rider can leave them feeling ignorant and demoralised. If the rider does not understand, be prepared to explain what you expect them to do in another way.

• Should the rider have problems with their horse, remain calm, and be empathetic and adaptable to the circumstances. You should not judge the rider, but have the resilience to repeat instructions, and assist them as much is required. Ending the lesson on a good note is essential, even if this means finishing before, or slightly after, the due time.

94. TEACHING STYLE

Aims of the exercise

The aim here is to evaluate teaching style in respect of teaching riding. One size does not fit all, and is influenced by the individuality of the teacher, and the learning style of students.

Step-by-step explanation of teaching style

Some teachers are naturally outgoing, others more reserved. In order to deliver lesson after lesson consistently, it is important that you are comfortable with your teaching style, which needs to reflect your knowledge and personality. Over time, you will develop your own style of teaching, being able to fulfil the brief of the training each individual requires while being mindful of your own needs and satisfaction as a teacher.

❑ There are different styles of teaching, which can be used either individually, or as part of an integrative teaching style. Instructing with an **authoritative style** involves giving instruction to students where they absorb information with little interaction. This is valuable for teaching an exercise, particularly in a group setting, or giving a lecture. To use this effectively, a depth of knowledge and confidence is required (*see* Exercise 93: Teacher Attributes).

❑ A **demonstrative** teacher shows student what they need to do by mannerisms, or by acting out what is required, which suits one-to-one sessions in which a personal approach is appreciated.

❑ Long-term students, who have a familiar rapport with their teacher, can benefit from a **facilitative** approach, as in coaching, which promotes self-learning and critical thinking. It requires interaction between you and your student(s), with each learning from the other. This approach requires prior knowledge by the student.

❑ Observing the group as a whole when working them together, such as working in open order, benefits from a **delegatory** approach.

Teaching Style	Strengths	Weaknesses	Areas to improve
Authoritative			
Demonstrative			
Facilitative			
Delegatory			
Integrative			

Using the self-assessment table, evaluate your teaching style.

❑ An **integrative** approach combines different teaching styles within a lesson, to fit best with student needs. However, there is a risk of losing focus on the goal of the session if you are not clear which approach you are using, and why, at any one time.

Common faults and how to rectify these

• Teaching can be tiring. Sitting down while instructing may be necessary, but it is vital to maintain focus on the rider and be fully engaged. It is a break for your body, not your mind.

• A disadvantage of a delegatory approach, working a group in open order, is a lack of authority. Unless riders have respect for the teacher, and control over their horses, the situation may become dangerous, with riders becoming confused as to how to keep a correct distance between each other. In this situation, maintain an air of authority to keep everybody safe.

95. TEACHING METHODS

Aims of the exercise

This exercise aims to give an understanding of different teaching methods in relation to riding.

Step-by-step explanation of teaching methods

A **direct teaching** method is systematic, **guided learning**, which lends itself to structured lessons. It is effective for teaching set principles, such as the scales of training, or giving a step-by-step explanation of a new exercise. With this style of teaching, questions are asked to assess what is understood, leading to immediate feedback and correction. It lends itself well to teaching novice riders.

❑ A **coaching** method supports **constructive learning**, in which pupils are supported as they learn for themselves, learning from experience what worked, what did not. This method is suited to more experienced riders who have already acquired the necessary skills to work with their horse. **Collaboration,** an aspect of coaching, is where a teacher (coach) and rider work as a team, for the good of the horse.

❑ **Interactive teaching** is working with feedback from the rider, asking questions as to their understanding of what is required, their sense of their horse, and their own riding skills. Use your observational skills to get a true sense of horse and rider, as to whether your teaching method is effective and well-received by the rider. Rider feedback enables you to adapt your teaching accordingly.

❑ A **combination method** of teaching (instructing) and coaching uses both structured and unstructured teaching in a single lesson. After structured teaching (instruction), using a direct method, the rider is asked to put their learning together in a single exercise to consolidate their learning, with the teacher acting as coach.

Teaching Methods	Strengths	Weaknesses	Areas to improve
Direct teaching			
Guided learning			
Coaching			
Constructive learning			
Interactive teaching			

Using the self-assessment table, evaluate your teaching methods.

Common faults and how to rectify these

• A downside of direct teaching is becoming set in your teaching style, using previously planned lessons. Take into consideration the individuality of students and adapt lessons accordingly.

• A negative interpretation of collaboration is where the rider becomes critical of your approach, and insisting on their own ideas being used. A less experienced teacher may say the rider is doing well, when in fact they are not. Remember you are not there to collude with the rider, but to coach.

• A pitfall of letting the rider work out an exercise for themselves, is the risk of things going wrong, and potentially causing an accident. Prompt intervention is required to prevent a loss of confidence on the rider's part, or a loss of trust between horse and rider.

96. PROFESSIONAL BOUNDARIES

Aims of the exercise

The aim here is to establish professional boundaries when teaching riding in order to keep the horse, rider and teacher all safe.

Step-by-step explanation of the exercise

For the teacher, professional boundaries are about maintaining a professional relationship with their pupil. This encompasses having regard for their appearance, wearing appropriate clothing, using terminology that the rider will understand, without being condescending, or 'blinding them with science'. A teacher should respect their student, be non-judgemental, and work with their best interests in mind.

❑ Safeguarding is part of a teacher's responsibility, having a duty of care for young riders. This involves making sure the actions, language and behaviour are non-offensive and appropriate for your pupil. Watching for signs of distress – caused by outside influences, such as home life and family relationships – comes under the remit of safeguarding. With adults, having an awareness of the student's wellbeing and state of mind, such as a lack of confidence or anxiety, impact on their ability to do well in their lesson, so it is important to keep this in mind.

❑ Boundaries between the teacher and student ensure a safe, productive lesson, so it is important for you to set 'house rules' with the rider. For example, it should be emphasised that the student must listen to, and respond to, instructions for their own safety, particularly with jumping.

❑ Confidentiality is key to keeping your student safe. Agreement must be made between teacher and client as to the permission, or not, of filming or photography by parents, friends, or the teacher and so on, and the intended use of such footage or photos.

Professional boundaries	Strengths	Weaknesses	Areas to improve
Teacher appearance, attitude			
House rules between teacher and student			
Safeguarding			
Handling outside influences			

Using the self-assessment table, evaluate your professional boundaries.

❑ Regarding the horse's welfare, have regard for the horse's fitness, stage of training, and relationship with its rider. Pushing horse and rider too far can cause injury or instil fear. Conversely, not challenging them enough limits their progress.

Common faults and how to rectify these

• Boundaries around the student's safety are familiar ground, but regard should also be had for your own safety, so make sure you are standing in a safe place in the arena. In extreme circumstances, where the rider has little control over their horse, then standing outside the arena would be a sensible option.

• Handling outside influences can be distracting for both teacher and rider, and undermine your authority. If there are spectators, it is useful to set boundaries at the beginning of the lesson to minimise interruptions, so you can do your job.

97. LESSON PLANNING

Aims of the exercise

The aim here is to assess the skills and strengths of horse and rider before training commences, which determines if the training is suitable for the level of horse and rider competence.

Step-by-step explanation of lesson planning

The more relevant information a teacher can glean from their student, the better. It will help you to modify your lesson accordingly, for the benefit of the rider and their horse. It is useful to have information about the rider's (and horse's) strengths and past achievements, and know what they enjoy in order to plan suitable training. Defining their goal for the lesson and what they want to achieve is important for a satisfactory outcome.

- During the initial assessment, you should be working out the teaching strategy – whether structured, or unstructured tuition – that would be the best for your student. This ensures horse and rider gain most benefit from their lesson.

- Structured lessons are formatted to teach specific skills. They can be one-off lessons, but are commonly part of a series of planned tuition. A beginning, middle and ending of each session is required. In a series of structured lessons, each lesson follows on from the one before, culminating in the end goal. (See the 'Training Plans' chapter.)

- Unstructured lessons are designed to develop skills that have already been learned. They take the form of a repeat of what the student has learned in structured lessons. The teacher should decide which lesson structure will bring out the best in their student.

- It is important to bear in mind the cognitive ability of the student, and not to overload them with information, nor to bore them with a lesson that is too simple.

Common faults and how to rectify these

- When teaching, it is important to take into account the learning style of students. Some

Assessing horse and rider competence	Strengths	Weaknesses	Areas to improve
Asking initial questions			
Recognising learning style			
Accessing fitness of horse and rider			
Lesson style structured/ unstructured			

Using the self-assessment table, evaluate your method of lesson planning.

students are visual learners, where they can replicate what they see. It helps to gesticulate, or demonstrate physically what is expected from the rider. In some circumstances, the rider will benefit from watching their horse being ridden, or observing another rider doing the same exercise. The best way to find out is to ask.

- Some riders benefit from listening to clear instructions, with the teacher talking them through an exercise, step by step.

- With riding being a physical activity, it is important to assess the physical fitness of both horse and rider, and noting their physical strengths. This might be of benefit to achieving skills and learning in the planned lesson.

TOP TIP

Utilising the strengths of both horse and rider to build on their existing experience leads to more confidence and a sense of achievement.

98. ASSESSING HORSE AND RIDER LIMITATIONS

Aims of the exercise

This exercise is about taking into account the rider's, and the horse's, limitations, which is essential for planning a suitable lesson to build their confidence.

Step-by-step explanation of assessing horse and rider limitations

Regarding the rider, limitations that could affect their learning progress could be physicality – namely their fitness level and physique – and their state of mind, such as their nervousness, and self-doubt. Limitations for the horse, affecting their response to the rider's aids, may well come from poor previous training, leading to incorrect musculature and a lack of trust in the rider. You may be faced with the less than perfect horse and rider combination, but it is your role to try to bring the best out in both.

❏ A skilled teacher engages their student by using their feedback to monitor how the lesson is progressing for them. This gives the rider the sense that the teacher is working in their best interest. Giving encouragement is key, as is a positive mindset and understanding in relation to what the rider finds difficult or frightening. For the teacher, being inclusive is about talking to the rider in such a way they do not feel they are the only rider struggling with a particular exercise. Being prepared to simplify the task they have set the rider, or break it down into manageable steps, leads to a sense of achievement.

❏ A rider's relationship with their horse can have a massive impact on their ability to engage in lessons. They may doubt the horse's willingness to listen to their aids, or be afraid it may spook, or they may fall off, especially if they have fallen from this particular horse previously.

Common faults and how to rectify these

• Taking into account the rider's cognitive learning limitations limits the risk of overloading the pupil with information. Being condescending, belittling the rider, or criticising their horse can destroy a rider's self-worth, so it is imperative to maintain

Assessing horse and rider limitations	Strengths	Weaknesses	Areas to improve
Ability to ask questions			
Being non-judgemental and empathic			
Developing a rapport			
Working with limitations of rider			
Working with limitations of horse			

Using the self-assessment table, evaluate your ability to work with horse and rider limitations.

a positive view of your student, giving plenty of encouragement and motivation to them.

• Past injuries and negative past experiences such as falling off can have a huge impact on the rider's confidence, so it is important to be non-judgemental and treat the rider with rider with empathy and understanding.

• It is human nature to remember bad experiences more clearly than good ones, so how the student remembers their teacher, and their learning experience, depends on developing a good rapport with them. Their trust in you may be affected by previous experiences as a child of being in a learning environment, such as school or a Pony Club. As adults, they may be limited by self-doubt and disappointment from poor competition results, or difficulties with their horse.

• Taking into account the limitations of horse and rider when planning a lesson leads to a sense of achievement for them, building on their confidence level.

99. SETTING CHALLENGES FOR HORSE AND RIDER

Aims of the exercise

How, and when, to challenge the horse and rider in training is key to their ability to rise to that challenge. The aim here is to discuss options.

Step-by-step explanation of setting challenges for horse and rider

The purpose of setting challenges for horse and rider is to test their skills, not to frighten them. A successful challenge is realistic, in that it is within their skill set, but takes their expertise to a higher level. The rider should be left feeling a sense of achievement, with an increased respect for their horse and pride in the outcome. A successful challenge improves the rapport between teacher and pupil, which bodes well for future challenges, in that the rider trusts your ability to get the best from them.

❏ Challenges are stepping stones throughout training, leading on to the next level of progress, taking the form of more complicated patterns, or a different combination of exercises. The rider may need to learn how to rise to the challenge. An example of introducing challenge in a lesson could be to improve their self-awareness by asking the rider to notice more, or feel more in their riding, focusing on more in-depth detail. They can be taught more equestrian terminology, for example replacing 'stop, go', with 'half-halt', or 'more oomph' with 'impulsion'.

❏ Their strengths should be used in order to develop confidence before stretching them, putting them out of their comfort zone. Giving support and encouragement is important, as learning is difficult, and the limitations of both horse and rider must also be taken into account.

Common faults and how to rectify these

• Realistic challenges should be set to test the rider's skills, not to frighten them. Not all riders respond in the same way to challenge, so it is important

Setting challenges	Strengths	Weaknesses	Areas to improve
Using challenge appropriately			
Defining challenge			
Using repetition			
Realistic expectations of horse and rider			

Using the self-assessment table, evaluate how you set challenges for horse and rider.

that their individuality is respected. Some rise to it, others less self-confident and in need of more reassurance. Be mindful of returning to an easier version of an exercise in order to always end on a good note, particularly if the rider, or horse, found it too difficult.

• The challenge set should be clearly defined, with instructions repeated as needed by the rider, to give them a sense that the challenge is possible and within their skill set.

• Be prepared to use reiteration in the lesson. It may seem too repetitive for you, having probably said the same thing over and over for years in your teaching career, but it is most likely the rider needs this replication in order to consolidate their learning.

• Learning comes from repetition, so you must be patient enough to work with this. It is important to have realistic expectations of horse and rider to avoid disappointment, and a loss of self-worth, for the rider. It helps if the rider has realistic expectations of their ability as well.

100. GIVING CONSTRUCTIVE CRITICISM ('FEEDBACK')

Aims of the exercise

To give constructive criticism – or 'feedback' – to the rider with the aim of broadening their awareness of areas to improve upon is the aim here.

Step-by-step explanation of giving constructive criticism

How you interact with your students is important, as this affects the way constructive criticism is delivered. A student who trusts their teacher will be able to take on board honest feedback in good heart, and learn more from it than a student with little respect for their teacher, and responds to criticism with disbelief.

❑ Constructive criticism aims to identify mistakes, and to help the rider to learn from their experience. Failure is necessary to learning: recognising the reasons for failure leads to the development of skills and expertise. Research shows that constructive criticism works best after an exercise is completed, by evaluating the student's performance and highlighting what could be improved upon next time. However, this may depend on the circumstance, with a rider needing direction from their coach as to the best way to approach an exercise.

❑ Your depth of knowledge and proficiency in delivering lessons is key to their student having faith that what they are being told is correct, and accepting constructive criticism. Use appropriate terminology – not attacking – be empathic, non-judgemental, supportive. Be clear and concise.

Common faults and how to rectify these

• Any criticism has the potential to be badly received, so this must be delivered with good intention and kindness. Care must be taken to deliver criticism factually and with fairness, but to be aware that students may react adversely to comments they may view as judgemental. Criticising a student should not be about belittling them, nor being arrogant.

Constructive criticism	Strengths	Weaknesses	Areas to improve
Relationship with student			
Expertise			
Evaluation ability			
Delivery of constructive criticism			

Using the self-assessment table, evaluate how you give constructive criticism.

• Taking into account that students respond individually to constructive criticism, the rider may need to learn how to accept constructive criticism if they have not experienced this before. In this case, appropriate terminology for the student's technical knowledge and level of training should be used. Blinding a rider with science leads to their confusion and self-doubt, and an adverse reaction to receiving feedback.

• Evaluating their own delivery of constructive criticism – such as tone of voice, posture and body language, including mannerisms – ensures that the teacher acts in the best interest of the student. Keeping critical comments short and to the point ensures they will be heard, as opposed to long-winded explanations that may fall on deaf ears. If criticism is not taken by the student, this wastes the time and effort of the teacher, which could leave both feeling despondent and dissatisfied with the outcome of the lesson.

When a lesson comes together it gives as much satisfaction to the teacher as the pupil.

HOW TO USE EXERCISES IN PRACTICE

SAFETY CONSIDERATIONS

Riding instructors have a duty of care to keep their clients safe. Health and safety guidance should be adhered to and a risk assessment carried out regarding premises used, type of lesson offered and potential incidents. Emergency procedures should be put in place, such as what to do if a rider falls off, or if one horse kicks another in a group lesson.

Another consideration is ending an unsafe lesson, or asking a rider to leave a group, should riders or horses be causing a risk to others. The safety of spectators must be taken into account, keeping them securely at a distance from any horses. Regarding personal risk, it is advisable for any client or spectator to complete a disclaimer.

A client registration form is helpful for the teacher to plan lessons in consideration of any issues either horse or rider may have that may affect their participation in a lesson. This is valuable for risk assessment.

For a freelance instructor, public liability insurance is required to give protection in case of an

Good ground conditions enable horse and rider to ride safely and accurately.

incident and riding instructor insurance covers teaching activities. Care, custody and control insurance covers negligent injury to a horse, and personal accident insurance for personal injury. A riding instructor employed by a stable yard will be covered by the yard insurance.

Belonging to a professional body, such as the British Horse Society (BHS), which offers insurance cover, is an option, and being a qualified instructor is usually a prerequisite for getting insurance. Anyone teaching children will be required to complete a safeguarding course. First aid at work certification is also required to be registered with the BHS.

For the teacher's own safety when teaching, they should position themselves out of harm's way, and wear suitable footwear and head protection. Horses are unpredictable, and it is not unknown for a teacher to be knocked over, kicked or bitten by a pupil's horse.

LESSON LOCATION: INDOOR SCHOOL; OUTDOORS; FIELD

When assessing lesson location, the safety of the environment and its suitability for the students should be taken into account. The doors to an indoor arena should shut securely, as should field gates. The ground, or arena surface, should be checked for evenness and degree of firmness to gauge if it is safe for the planned lesson. The vicinity should be inspected for potential hazards that may frighten horses or riders, from a health and safety perspective: these might include other animals being close by, traffic, chain saws in operation, building works, helicopters overhead and so on. A contingency should be made for bad weather and deteriorating ground conditions.

INDIVIDUAL LESSONS

The advantage of individual lessons is that they can be tailor-made to suit the requirements of rider and horse. One-to-one lessons can be intense, though, and care should be taken to monitor the rider's ability to stay focused, with plenty of short breaks between exercises if they tire. This type of lesson, suited to both coaching/direct teaching styles, can also be draining for the teacher, so self-care is required, particularly when teaching for several hours.

SHARED LESSONS (TWO RIDERS)

It is important to share time fairly between two riders, and to determine whether a coaching or direct teaching style is appropriate.

Managing a lesson in which the horses and riders are of the same level of experience is more straightforward than if they are of differing standards. No favouritism should be shown, which can be challenging if one rider demands more attention – by asking lots of questions, perhaps. One student may show off to the other, so care is needed to manage both riders, so that the other does not feel left out.

A lesson may be shared by two riders that know each other, or a pair that do not, which will impact on how a rapport is built with the teacher. Finding out if the horses know each other determines how close the riders can work in proximity to each other.

GROUP LESSONS

When working with a group of riders, for a successful lesson in which everyone feels they have benefited, it is important to keep all pupils engaged and to teach at a level at which all riders can participate. This setting suits an authoritative (direct) teaching style (see Teaching Style: Exercise 94). Teaching a group requires using general comments, so as not to single anyone out, which could make them feel self-conscious.

Assessing the group as to whether they are used to working together – perhaps the horses are in a riding school situation, or it is a group of riders and horses that do not know each other – helps the teacher to manage the situation. One option for group work is in single file as a ride, determining which order the horses should be in and which rider is best as lead/rear file to keep the pace suitable for all. Quadrille riding, in formation, requires a teacher good at being directive and keeping order, which may involve asking riders to leave the arena if they are disturbing the group.

With a group that does not know each other involving a maximum of eight riders, dividing them into two smaller groups – working at each end of the arena on a 20m-diameter circle, four on each circle – can be useful in terms of keeping them all at a safe distance from one another. The circles must work on the same rein to avoid head-on collisions over X.

TRAINING PLANS: COMBINING EXERCISES TOGETHER TO CREATE A LESSON THEME

Exercises can be combined across all groups, with novice exercises being a preparation for intermediate and advanced exercises, and a check that basic riding principles are being adhered to in more advanced exercises.

Lesson Theme						
Transitions	Exercise 31 Stretching	Exercise 4 Transitions	Exercise 22 Dressage Letters	Exercise 32 Transitions	Exercise 82 Cones for Transitions	Exercise 2 Stretching
Jumping a Grid	Exercise 11 Establishing Jumping Position	Exercise 16 Trotting Poles with a Fence	Exercise 45 Trotting Poles with a Double Fence	Exercise 76 Double Fence from Canter	Exercise 79 Jumping Grid	Exercise 20 Cool-Down for Jumping
Bend	Exercise 31 Stretching	Exercise 7 Circles 20m Diameter	Exercise 9 Figure of Eight	Exercise 6 Changes of Rein	Exercise 54 Cones for Double Loops	Exercise 51 Stretching
Lateral Work	Exercise 21 Warm-Up	Exercise 8 Single loops	Exercise 56 Cones for Turn on the Forehand	Exercise 39 Leg Yield	Exercise 36 Shoulder-In	Exercise 2 Stretching
Straightness	Exercise 31 Stretching	Exercise 3 Straight Lines	Exercise 34 Changes of Rein	Exercise 27 Poles for Straight Lines	Exercise 88 Poles for Rein-Back	Exercise 10 Work on a Long Rein
Collection Extension	Exercise 21 Warm-Up	Exercise 5 Corners	Exercise 6 Changes of Rein	Exercise 66 Half-Pass	Exercise 62 Collection/ Extension	Exercise 31 Stretching
Jumping a Course	Exercise 12 Warm-Up	Exercise 17 Single Jumps From Trot	Exercise 43 Perfecting Lines of Approach	Exercise 73 Difficult Lines of Approach	Exercise 49 Simple Course in Canter	Exercise 50 Cool-Down
Flying Changes	Exercise 21 Warm-Up	Exercise 8 Single Loops	Exercise 29 Poles for Figures of Eight	Exercise 59 Poles for Three-Loop Serpentine	Exercise 67 Flying Changes	Exercise 10 Work on a Long Rein
Half-Pass Zigzags	Exercise 2 Stretching	Exercise 37 Double Loops	Exercise 85 Poles for Travers	Exercise 66 Half-Pass	Exercise 84 Cones for Half-Pass Zigzags	Exercise 50 Cool Down
Riding a Dressage Test	Exercise 21 Warm-Up	Exercise 29 Poles for Figures of Eight	Exercise 32 Transitions	Exercise 61 10m Circles	Exercise 89 Combination Props for Accuracy	Exercise 31 Stretching
Jumping Single Fences	Exercise 12 Warm-Up for Jumping	Exercise 17 Single Jumps from Trot	Exercise 44 Trotting Poles with a Single Fence	Exercise 74 Canter Poles with an Upright Fence	Exercise 75 Canter Poles with a Spread Fence	Exercise 20 Cool-down for Jumping
Jumping a Double	Exercise 72 Warm-Up	Exercise 43 Perfecting Lines of Approach	Exercise 45 Trotting Poles with a Double Fence	Exercise 76 Double Fence from Canter	Exercise 78 Two-Stride Double	Exercise 50 Cool-Down

CONCLUSION

Teaching riding exercises is about delivering interesting and engaging lessons, appropriate to the level or training of both horse and rider. As well as improving the student, the dedicated teacher will constantly strive to evaluate – and develop – their lesson delivery technique throughout their teaching career.

I hope, through working through this book, that teachers will feel inspired to be creative in their work and in their own training. A riding instructor's sense of vocation needs to be resilient to keep going when riders are frightened, disappointed or overwhelmed by self-doubt, but helping students achieve their goals in life can be exciting and rewarding. (If you have read this book as a rider, I hope it has helped to put into perspective the intricacies of planning suitable training for you and your horse.)

As a teacher, self-belief and confidence develop from being a valued contributor to the progress of horse and rider, and the importance of recognising your own areas of expertise embracing your individuality and your own unique teaching style is not to be underestimated. Good teachers are worth their weight in gold and deserve to be valued – not only by their students, but by their peers, and also by themselves.

Attention to detail helps the rider to perfect their riding position.

REFERENCES

British Dressage handbook (2022) (online version). Available at: https://edition.pagesuite-professional.co.uk/html5/reader/production/defaultaspx?pubname=&pubid=7b196635-543f-4a72-950b-7f3adc71c7c8 (accessed 7 January 2022)

Gill, E. (2020) 'What is your teaching style? Five effective teaching methods for your classroom.' *Resilient educator: Tips for teachers and classroom resources* (online). Available at: https://resilienteducator.com/classroom-resources/5-types-of-classroom-teaching-styles/ (accessed 7 January 2022)

Light, D. (2017) 'Stretch and challenge in your classroom.' *Resilient educator: Tips for teachers and classroom resources* (online). Available at: https://resilienteducator.com/classroom-resources/5-types-of-classroom-teaching-styles/ (accessed 7 January 2022)

Morgan, S. (2016) 'Maintaining your professional boundaries.' *Seced: the voice for secondary education.* Available at: https://www.sec-ed.co.uk/best-practice/maintaining-your-professional-teaching-boundaries-1/ (accessed 7 January 2022)

Stringer, H. (2021). 'Constructive criticism that works.' *Monitor on Psychology*, 52 (7). Available at: http://www.apa.org/monitor/2021/10/career-constructive-criticism (accessed 7 January 2022)

University of Minnesota (2022) *Advance your teaching, engage your learners* (online). Available at: https://cei.umn.edu/writing-your-teaching-philosophy (accessed 7 January 2022)

Westwood, P. (2008) *What teachers need to know about teaching methods.* Victoria, Australia: Acer Books

RELATED TITLES AVAILABLE FROM J.A. ALLEN